The Land Army's
Lost Women

The Land Army's Lost Women

Emily Ashworth

For my children, Maggie May and Henry Victor,
for my family whom I owe everything to, and for my angels

PEN & SWORD
HISTORY

First published in Great Britain in 2023 by
Pen & Sword History
An imprint of
Pen & Sword Books Ltd
Yorkshire – Philadelphia

Copyright © Emily Ashworth 2023

ISBN 978 1 52678 545 9

Typeset by Mac Style
Printed in the UK by CPI Group (UK) Ltd, Croydon, CR0 4YY.

MIX
Paper | Supporting
responsible forestry
FSC
www.fsc.org   FSC® C013604

Pen & Sword Books Limited incorporates the imprints of Atlas,
Archaeology, Aviation, Discovery, Family History, Fiction, History,
Maritime, Military, Military Classics, Politics, Select, Transport, True
Crime, Air World, Frontline Publishing, Leo Cooper, Remember
When, Seaforth Publishing, The Praetorian Press, Wharncliffe Local
History, Wharncliffe Transport, Wharncliffe True Crime, White Owl
and After the Battle.

For a complete list of Pen & Sword titles please contact

PEN & SWORD BOOKS LIMITED
47 Church Street, Barnsley, South Yorkshire, S70 2AS, England
E-mail: enquiries@pen-and-sword.co.uk
Website: www.pen-and-sword.co.uk

Or

PEN AND SWORD BOOKS
1950 Lawrence Rd, Havertown, PA 19083, USA
E-mail: Uspen-and-sword@casematepublishers.com
Website: www.penandswordbooks.com

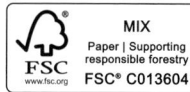

Contents

For you Grandma …

I remember how when you would tell me a story, your eyes would be so bright and alive as though you were seeing it playing out in front of you. Your words were so full of colour, your laughter a short gasp of pure joy at whatever tale was left in your wake. I hope I can tell these stories like that. I hope they jump from the page and inspire at least one person to remember what you and many others did for us.

I love you.

And I know we'll meet again, some sunny day …

Back to the land, we must all lend a hand
To the farms and the fields we must go.
There's a job to be done
Though we can't fire a gun
We can still do our bit with a hoe.
When your muscles are strong
You will soon get along
And you'll think that the country life's grand;
We're all needed now,
We must speed with the plough,
So come with us – back to the land.

Official Land Army song, 1942

Harvesting flax on a farm in Huntingdonshire during 1942. (*Wikimedia*)

Introduction

When you lose a grandparent, it is a very strange feeling. Strange because you know it is coming, especially as they start to live into their eighties and nineties, and I have been lucky enough to have had two grandmothers who, after living a life filled with grandchildren, great grandchildren and great-great grandchildren, reached such ages. Despite this, the pain is inevitable. Knowing it is going to happen does not make it any easier, nor does it make the grieving process simpler. In fact, for me it was harder to come to terms with as I was fortunate enough to spend thirty years of my life with these women, both of whom were born in 1926, lived through some extraordinary times and faced their own battles during those years.

My farming history is on my dad's side, and it was his mother, Vera, my grandma Ashworth, who inspired this particular book after becoming a Land Girl in 1944 in Lancashire. When I lost her in 2017 I really struggled, more so because I had recently been blessed with motherhood for the first time. I will never forget how happy she was when I brought my daughter to meet her. In fact, I named my daughter Maggie May after my grandmothers, Margaret and Vera May. When you place a newborn into your grandparents' arms, the image of time truly hits you – their defiance of age, their fragility. I was always chatting to her about her life, and in the throes of her stories I could not help but be in awe of what this woman before me must have seen and sacrificed. Do not get me wrong, she was one of the lucky ones and had a great innings, but I struggled with the fact that my daughter would never hug her again. I struggled knowing I would never sit there and listen to her stories or hear her break into spontaneous song.

I still believe that part of her longevity was down to lots of fresh air, a lifetime of being outdoors on the farm and good food. Yes, my grandma, Vera May Whyte Ashworth (née Flemming), was a strong lady, known for her abrupt demeanour, and her straight-talking ways were renowned in our village. But when you look at what she went through, when you immerse yourself in the hardship she faced from living through the war to bringing up five children on a farm that was not profitable, I think her somewhat icy exterior could perhaps be forgiven.

To me, however, she was nothing but warm. I know wholeheartedly that she saw parts of herself in me. And, given that she was never one for going out, I was maybe a kind of social saviour for her. I have always had a unique obsession with the past, and grandma lived in her memories. We fitted together quite nicely. As a young girl I guess it was quite unusual for an eight-year-old to sit there and revel in her old grandma's wafflings from World War Two, but something resonated with me. And so, when she got the chance to talk, she went hell-for-leather on the tale-telling.

Her life had been an incredible one. She was a heroine in my eyes and when she died at the grand age of ninety, I knew immediately that her story must be told – not just to honour her, but to make sure that future women know what thousands of women in the past had done to enable us to live the way we do. I think the most poignant quote you can live by, considering today's battle for gender equality and political stability, are Theodore Roosevelt's words, 'the more you know about the past, the better prepared you are for the future.'

And so, the idea for the book was created, and although evolving from the despair I was feeling about my grandma's passing, it has taken on a life-form of its very own. I wanted to collate a book of personal memoirs; a collection of stories from Land Girls that simply showed these women for what they were – young and brave; funny and smart; selfless and caring. I found that their downfall was their image – farming does not call for glamour, yet I know my grandma was glamorous and I feel compelled to create a different view of these women.

Every woman I met had similarities to my grandma and I will never forget how comforting that felt. To know that as I was helping them by telling their stories, they were unknowingly helping me heal.

Meeting former members did, of course, help me deal with my loss, but it also ignited another fire within me, one which I did not even know was gently burning: the issues of women's equality, women's pay, the image of women through time, and women's choices. You would think that in the time that has passed the gender balance in society would have

700 members voice their grievances in London demanding equal pay for equal work. (*Wikimedia*)

reached an equilibrium, that the conversation surrounding pay equality and fair parental maternity and paternity packages would have become unnecessary. But we are still battling, still questioning, and still facing prejudice in some cases, just like the Women's Land Army.

As welcoming as many were to the Land Girls, equally as many objected to women taking on what was considered male work. There are quotes in the Land Girl voluntary manual that record farmers' reactions to being landed with women on their farms, and their surprise at their ability. One, attributed only to 'A Hexham farmer, reads:

> As you know, I was very doubtful about the wisdom of taking two girls who had had no previous experience. My fears were quite groundless. They have been quick to learn, and have worked hard at all manner of tasks – not a few of them both dirty and uncongenial. I have nothing but praise for them.

Despite their willingness to plunge themselves in to a male-dominated environment and prove themselves worthy, so many of these women have said that had it not been for me telling their stories, many would not have heard of the Women's Land Army. So, my second reason for writing these memoirs came down to the shocking lack of knowledge about this branch of the women's forces during the war, plus the lack of recognition in the following years. There is obviously an endless list of females to champion throughout history, but still, for some obscure reason, the Women's Land Army are mostly left to champion their own efforts.

Lastly, I found that former members who were still living would never be remembered for what they did had someone not taken the time to preserve their memoirs. How can we learn from one of the greatest female sacrifices in our recent history if we do not listen?

I know the kind of woman I want my own daughter to look up to, and that is one of strength, determination, relentless fight and hard work. I wanted to create a different image of the Women's Land Army too; one that made them accessible to the women of today, to shine a more modern light on them rather than simply casting them to the side as dowdy farm hands, which was certainly not the case.

Today, as an agricultural journalist, I know there are more women than ever in the farming industry, undertaking all sorts of roles. Our sector is probably the most vibrant it has ever been, and we have also witnessed our own historic moment within farming as Minette Batters became the first ever female President of the National Farmers Union. If you look back, the last time there was a large percentage of women in the industry was probably during World War Two.

Without the help of family and friends, and from those willing to send me countless books, written accounts and photographs, I could not have done it. I thank you all for that, from the bottom of my heart.

When I first put the idea out there, the response was quite overwhelming – I found people wanted to know more, which surprised and pleased me. I spoke to women my age, in their twenties and thirties, who said how interested they were in my project and could not wait to read it. Yet, for so many years, we never spoke of them or heard of them during our school years – nothing specifically memorable anyway.

As you will read, the most popular image of women from wartime that springs to most people's minds first are from the various glamourous posters – not women on a farm in their britches. I have always wondered if we were put in the same situation today would we be able to muster up such communal spirit and take on backbreaking work like they did? It is an understatement to say that some of these women were completely out of their comfort zone – some gladly, some not so.

While writing this book I have myself witnessed a world crisis. 2020 saw me give birth to my second child, Henry Victor, born on Victory in Europe day would you believe, at the height of a pandemic. The world shut down for over a year while world leaders tried to navigate its people through the havoc caused by the deadly Coronavirus as it swept through our lives. On 23 March 2020 we were put into lockdown, only able to leave our homes for food shopping and essential work. Children stayed home, exams were cancelled, and pregnant women like me were made to attend appointments alone – some even giving birth alone. It was said to be one of the biggest national crises since the Second World War.

The two, of course, are not comparable, but I have learned that inner strength and mindset are vital to weather any storm, and had my grandma been alive to witness this epidemic, she would have been confined to the four walls of her granny flat and would have done what she had to with no fuss. I have no doubt about that. There is a reason the popular saying, 'they don't make them like that anymore' has lasted – it is because they do not.

Something that also struck me was the fact that, yet again, just like in the Second World War, we must ask the question: which industry kept us going? Farming. Food production is paramount and without those who work tirelessly – pandemic, war, crises aside – the value of those who produce our food is of the utmost importance. For me this really highlights the significance of the Land Girls' effort.

Every single member I have had the honour of speaking to has distinct traits that I cannot help but notice; innate and almost inbuilt in them but all characteristics women should be allowed to have. Like my own grandmother, these former members have shown defiance, strong-will, iron determination and not one iota of self-pity, especially when it comes to how downplayed their contribution was. These are not aggressive or over-bearing qualities: they are features I think sometimes we as women are perhaps a little afraid to have. This is slowly changing, but still being challenged. Knowing your own mind, pushing yourself to the limit and having the ability to sacrifice for a greater cause are attractive attributes and ones to be proud of. They are certainly things I would like to highlight about the women in a period of history that connects us all.

I hope to be able to prove that these women deserve a celebrated place in history because there is always a reason to celebrate strong women.

It was, however, also about the land, and the love they had for it. I cannot speak for every single land girl, but many speak of the countryside so beautifully, as if it became part of them, especially for those who married into this way of life.

Farmers have an intrinsic connection to the land they tend, and dispersed throughout this book are some of the poems written by Land Girls – taken from *Poems of the Land Army* – many of which evoke all sorts of emotions, but all of which capture farm life through the seasons and through wartime perfectly.

These poems are both humorous and heartfelt, witty yet heartbreaking at times. But they completely encompass the reality of their new life, working from dusk until dawn, and of taking the opportunity to finally gain independence and freedom, even under the constraints of wartime. The following verse is striking:

Land Girl collecting hay from the stack to feed cattle at the WLA training centre at Cannington in Somerset. (*Wikimedia*)

War, which has brought to others fear,
Pain, sorrow, slavery, and death
To me has brought what I held dear
And longed for but could not possess.

Vita Sackville-West, who wrote the foreword for *Poems of the Land Army*, highlights an important point regarding these words, and this was so true for many of these women:

> the note of their own liberation into a more congenial life. How often one has heard a land-girl say that nothing would induce her to return to a "cooped up existence"; so here among the poets one naturally looks for the expression of feeling and, explicit or implicit, one finds it.

For the love of farming, for the love of their country, for the love of the women working beside them, and their freedom, each one immersed themselves into this new life wholeheartedly.

Land girls in Devon. Left to right: Grace Foster (aged 21, from Colchester), Penny Arberry (aged 19, from Plymouth), Ellen Howe (driving, aged 18 from Tooting in London) and Jackie Crane (aged 18 from Stoke Newington in London). (*Wikimedia*)

A talk about rats in the pig sty. (*Wikimedia*)

Women training at Cannington farm in Somerset around 1940. (*Wikimedia*)

Soon we will be in a position where veterans – men and women – from the Second World War will be sadly gone, and our generation will only be left with the stories. We must make sure that what the Women's Land Army did continues to be acknowledged more and more, and ensure we view their contribution as more than just women who 'stood in the place of men'.

These were women who rose to the challenge; women who conquered the task despite oppressed adversity.

These were women who helped to win the war.

Farmer Tuppin showing girls how to trap rats. (*Wikimedia*)

Timeline of Events

June 1939 – The Women's Land Army is reinstated to ensure a national food shortage is prevented.

September 1939 – Britain declares war on Germany.

January 1940 – Food rationing begins in Britain.

April 1940 – A monthly magazine *The Land Girl* is published by the Women's Land Army, with Margaret Pyke as its editor.

May 1941 – All women aged between nineteen and forty must register for war work.

December 1941 – By Autumn of 1941, over 20,000 women had volunteered. But by December, conscription was introduced.

April 1942 – The Women's Timber Corps (WTC) is formed. The WTC worked in forestry to build timber supplies.

June 1942 – In order to provide financial assistance to Land Girls who suffered injuries or illness due to their work, Lady Denham starts The Land Army Benevolent Fund.

August 1943 – The War Cabinet decides to stop recruiting for the Women's Land Army given that more workers were needed in the aircraft production industry.

August 1943 – Women's Land Army correspondence courses in agriculture and horticulture and proficiency tests begin. These tests are introduced to measure and recognise Land Girls' agricultural skills such as spreading manure, sugar beet pulling and the identification of plants and weeds.

January 1944 – Recruitment to the Women's Land Army reopens.

July 1944 – The first series of Proficiency Tests are completed.

January 1945 – Land Girls who have been in the Land Army for three or more years are given special consideration and are able to request transfers to their home counties.

February 1945 – The decision to exclude members of the Land Girls from post-war financial benefits causes Lady Denham to resign.

May 1945 – Victory in Europe Day marks the end of war in Europe.

November 1950 – The Women's Land Army is disbanded.

'The Milky Way'

Inez M. Jenkins, Chief administrative Officer, Women's Land Army

"I wonder," said the Land Girl,
 I wonder," said the cow;
"It can't be hard," the Land Girl said,
"The only thing is *how*,
"And will she kick me if I try?"
"I wonder," said the cow.

"Oh bother!" cried the Land Girl,
"Why bother?" cried the cow;
"Why can't you let the matter drop?
 I just can't face it now.
 You'll dry me off. I know you will!
 Oh, *bother*!" cried the cow.

"It's not too bad," the Land Girl said,
"It's bad," replied the cow;
"Shove over there," the Land Girl said,
"We needn't have a row.
 There now, we're doing nicely, see!"
"Not bad," replied the cow.
"Nice milk," remarked the Land Girl.
"Too kind!" remarked the cow.
 The Land Girl curtsied by her stool,
 The cow essayed a bow.
 Sweet harmony thus reigned between
 The Land Girl and the cow.

Iris Joyce, 1942. (*Wikimedia*)

Who Were the Women's Land Army?

Put simply, The Women's Land Army were an organisation of women who took on agricultural labour during wartime, filling the space left by the thousands of men who had gone to fight.

First coming to fruition in World War One, The Women's Land Army was primarily established by The British Board of Agriculture, under its director Meriel Talbot in 1917, and accomplished the task set out before it: to feed the nation and keep the agricultural cogs of Britain turning. But, just twenty years later, as the country prepared itself to fight once more, in the months before war was declared on Germany plans to reform the Women's Land Army had begun. World War One saw food supplies in dire straits, and measures were put in place to ensure agricultural stability once more.

Meriel set the precedent first time around, establishing the key difficulties and ways to overcome them in order to encourage women into the branch and allow things to proceed as efficiently as possible.

These were:

- The source of supply – many women had already been drafted into other forces;
- The scepticism of farmers – it was also a case of overcoming the general public's scepticism;
- The problem of waiting time – this looked at the time between training, testing and employment;
- The wages to be paid – Land Army wages depended on the individual farmer, not the government, as with other women's services;
- The question of billeting;
- The loneliness of farm work – there is a noteworthy difference here between other women's services and those enrolled in the Women's Land Army. For those that worked the land, although

some worked together, many were posted individually on farms. Even today, loneliness is a huge factor in farming, and there are issues associated with being so isolated.

Second time around, its founding member, Lady Gertrude Mary Denman, was a fierce women's right's activist, executive of the Women's Liberal Federation and the first President of the National Federation of Women's Institutes, a post she held until 1946.

Nicola Tyrer, in her book *They Fought In The Fields* describes Lady Denman, saying, 'she too remembered the beleaguered city of 1917 – and the procrastinating patronising attitude of the politicians and civil servants she had to deal with was striking. She grasped, in a way they seem unable to, the central role the WLA would need to play in winning the war.'

But it is Lady Denman's statement that probably encompasses the true Women's Land Army spirit: 'The land army fights in

Lady Gertrude Mary Denman. (*Wikimedia*)

the fields. It is in the fields of Britain that the most critical battle of the present war may well be fought and won.'

Information on the Women's Land Army in the National Service Handbook, 1939, reads:

In the event of war a Women's Land Army will be organised. This body will be a mobile force consisting of women who are ready to undertake all kinds of farm work in any part of the country. The members will wear uniform, although they will normally be employed and paid by individual farmers, and the organisation will supervise their lodging arrangements and general welfare. There will also be a need for women who are only able to offer their services for work in their home district.

The truth of the matter was that Britain could not have fed itself had there been nobody to work the land, and without the Land Girls our nation would have faced starvation. With German blockades stopping imports and most of the country's male agricultural workforce on the frontline, Britain would have been forced into submission. The cry for women workers to journey back to Britain's countryside was overwhelming.

In 1938 Lady Denham, a self-confessed feminist who had already helped to change the WI's 'Jam and Jerusalem' façade, was approached by the Ministry of Agriculture to once again start planning the recruitment of women to work within the farming industry. It was an incredibly extensive task, and to successfully execute arrangements that were so widely spread across the country was no mean feat.

This element, says Cherish Watton, founder of the award-winning Women's Land Army website and PhD candidate in Modern British History at Churchill College, Cambridge, is one that is severely overlooked. It seems that the branch was viewed as one that was, perhaps, less important than other war work carried out by women. But this could also be due to the fact that the Women's Land Army was a civilian organisation and not military.

Cherish says:

> I think generally there has been a delay of recognition because they were working in a civilian occupation and there was more attention focused on women working in the armed forces.

There was constant tension with the Women's Land Army being called an "army".

> But I also think there's a wider history of agriculture being ignored. There were women working on the land before the land girls and it's taken a long while for those perspectives to come through. So, there is a wider neglect of agricultural work and effort.

I have read so much that has celebrated female roles in the armed forces, such as The Women's Royal Naval Service, the Women's Auxiliary Air Force and the Auxiliary Territorial Service, calling them 'vital'. They almost always go on to talk of the Women's Land Army as simply an addition to these and not a separate branch that was of equivalence in service. Surely one of the most crucial tasks of all was to ensure that Britain did not starve itself into surrender?

Once, in a BBC radio broadcast, Miss Clemence Dane, a playwright and novelist, referred to the Women's Land Army as the 'Cinderella Service', alluding to commonly-held views about its inferior status and, more critically, overlooking its importance.

After the war Land Girls were also excluded from post-war financial benefits, thus further demonstrating how their contribution was overlooked.

The evidence does pay tribute to their efforts, though. Before the war, seventy percent of the country's food was imported, and due to German barricades and the threat to ships, Britain had to look to its own farmers to do what we now know as the term 'grow your own'.

Incredibly, with the work of the Women's Land Army, that ratio was almost all but reversed by the end of the war, proof of how integral these women were to keep the engine of Britain turning.

In *Land Girl*, a handbook which was created as a sort of practical guide for those about to become Land Girls, it says: 'The Land Army must have a motto – *Stick to It.*'

It goes on to say: 'Every volunteer should remember that money has been spent on her equipment and training, to make her a specialist for a vital job. She should not, therefore, ever drop out [...] She must feel like she is feeding the nation. If she drops out, someone may starve.'

It was a serious consideration to become a Land Girl. At its peak in 1944 over 80,000 women became part of the WLA, with a further 10,000 acting as Lumberjills – women who joined The Women's Timber Corps, an even lesser-known branch but also of equal great importance. The Timber Corps carried out forestry tasks, providing wood materials for necessities such as railway tracks, telegraph poles and, more sadly, coffins.

From the beginning of the Second World War to the disbandment of the Land army in 1950, over 200,000 women became Land Girls. That is a lot of women to allow time to forget – my grandma along with them.

It is also somewhat unimaginable to conceive that many of these women had never seen a farm animal or even set foot in the Great British countryside. Many confessed to having no clue about what they were doing, or if they were doing it right.

Land girls using
a double saw
at a training
camp in Suffolk.
(*Wikimedia*)

Moving cut timber in Welshpool. (*Wikimedia*)

The diversity in its members is, however, what I believe to be one of the most outstanding factors about the organisation. So many different personalities and social classes were thrown together. I particularly enjoyed hearing former members express their disbelief that so many women came together from such contrasting backgrounds: miners' daughters, schoolgirls, hairdressers, teachers, and, like my grandma, those from the fashion world or the West End. You name it, there was every type of character from every type of family, social class or occupation, none of this was of any regard when it came to gathering girls. Perhaps this is something we can draw on today, in a society that aims to become more accepting of one another in every way possible.

I have not yet come across any former members who have told me they did not either enjoy their time or gain something from the whole experience, though there were times when I thought that looking back on their journey probably made them see things differently. Maybe the passing of time allows you to mellow and become more accepting.

Their days were excruciatingly long, arduous and rough, yet not one of them expressed any anger or resentment. Perhaps a sense of pride in what they were doing was enough to carry them through? Or maybe I have reached out to them too late and there is no bad feeling left to harbour.

* * *

Until 1941 the service was purely voluntary, encouraging young, single women to volunteer. But as dark war clouds gathered women became indispensable, and conscription was introduced. Anyone aged from nineteen up to forty years old were called upon to sign up to carry out war work of various natures including munitions work and air raid wardens. Probably the best-known roles are those such as The Women's Royal Naval Service, the Women's Auxiliary Air Force and the Auxiliary Territorial Service – with perhaps the most notable member of the Auxiliary Service being Queen Elizabeth II.

The recruitment posters for the Women's Land Army gave the impression of rosy country living, plastered with slogans such as 'For a healthy, happy job join the Women's Land Army', which also perhaps helped to attract those living in urban areas. The women on these posters were smiling, bright-eyed and looked as though they were enjoying every second of life out in the countryside. Quite a few of the women I have interviewed have confessed they were drawn in by such images, but swiftly found that it was not always the reality.

It must have been a daunting experience to be plucked from anywhere and sent to the heart of the British countryside with, as I have since learnt, no training, no family and no support, to learn how to milk, how to plough and even how to drive. The latter is a part of our everyday lives that we take for granted, but it would have been a luxury for most women

Recruitment posters for the WLA. (*Wikimedia*)

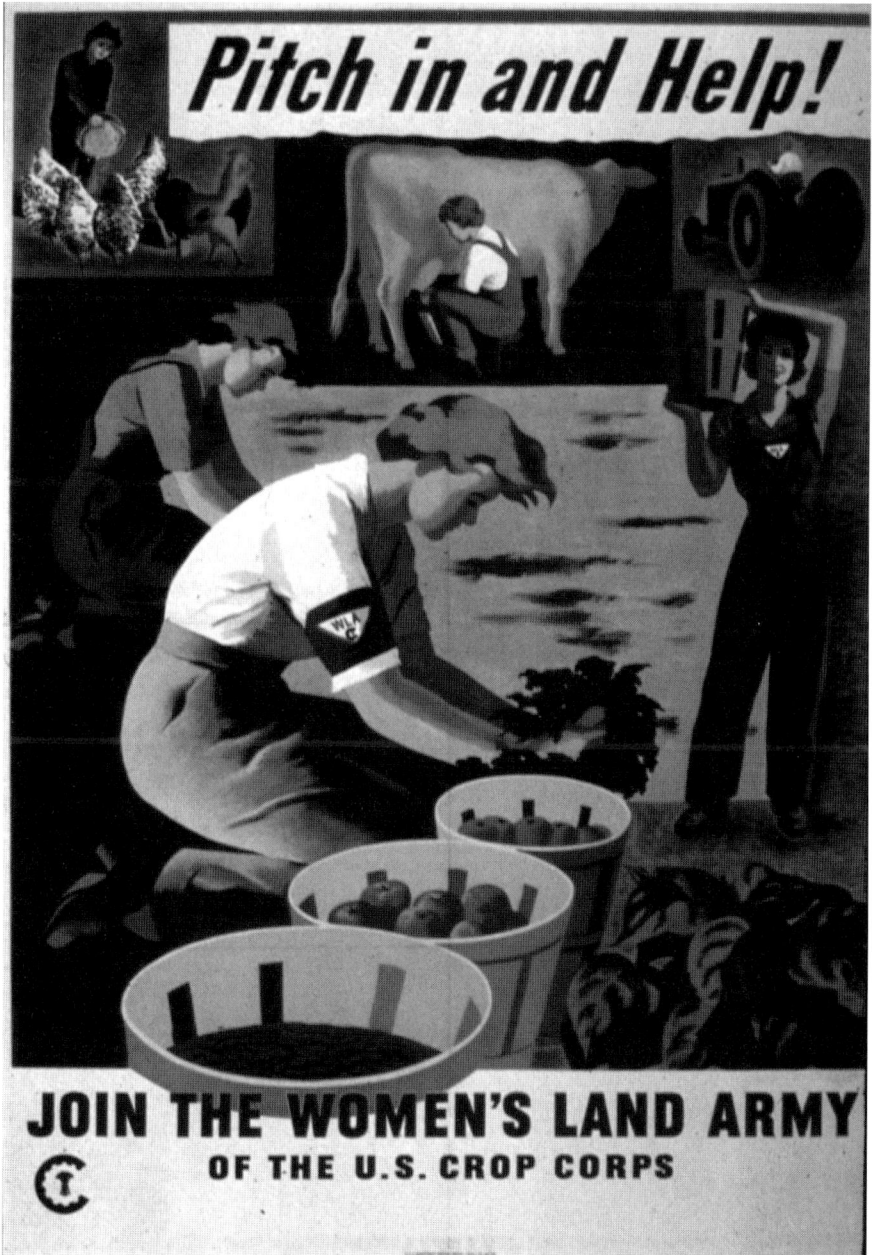

These posters tried to show women a happy life in the countryside. (*Wikimedia*)

Many were drawn in by what the recruitment posters offered. (*Wikimedia*)

Women from all walks of life were needed. (*Wikimedia*)

of that era. So many have said that this was their main reason for joining up, the chance to drive. Otherwise, such opportunities would not have come their way.

Those who were not housed in hostels were placed with families. For many, these people became a home from home, but some were not always warm and welcoming. Cherish says:

> You do hear that their time in the land army was the best of their lives. Having that independence and moving away; meeting new women, new men – American men, Italian or German POWs, members of the rural communities.
>
> For other women who were alone and isolated on a farm, it could be an incredibly lonely experience. You do hear stories of farmers taking advantage of them, such as giving them the worst cow to milk for the first time when they haven't been given any training.
>
> You do also hear of cases of sexual harassment, even though this isn't spoken of much.
>
> If you were isolated, there wasn't really a great deal you could do. I have heard cases of the farmer's wives taking the ration cards from the land girl and not necessarily giving her the food she was entitled to. If you haven't got the food to keep you going that is obviously a big problem when you're doing so much physical work. You could just feel very excluded.

In a bid to try and alleviate the worry of isolation and loneliness, a magazine was created, *The Land Girl*, first published in April 1940. It began as an unofficial Land Army document, but after selling 21,000 copies per week the ministry of agriculture funded its production.

Within their groups, however, women formed unbreakable bonds that have lasted a lifetime. It was about women working together, lifting each other during their darkest times and proving that by collectively pursuing the same goal success was inevitable.

Working roles were also varied in the Women's Land Army. Some were part of mobile gangs, shipped at short notice from place to place, while others were stationed on their own, in groups on specific farms, or worked as market gardeners.

Land girls digging up turnips. (*Wikimedia*)

Although general farm work was naturally expected, other aspects of farm life came as a shock to many. For example, women were sometimes employed as rat catchers on farm, with the most common memory probably of Land Army members having to tie up the bottoms of their trousers to stop pests running up their legs. The line was, 'Kill That Rat: It's Doing Hitler's Work', a propaganda statement to encourage those of a more squeamish nature.

In 1943 proficiency tests were introduced which assessed women in specific farming skills. The criteria covered the following areas: milk and dairy work; general farm work; poultry and tractor driving; field work; outdoor garden and glasshouse work; and fruit work and pest destruction. Members were able to don a badge of proficiency if they scored seventy-five per cent or above, a small accolade of their work and capability.

Speaking to some of the last living Land Army members, the farming industry they speak of seems like a world away, where pretty much everything was manually done. Consider how mechanised farming and food production is today – technology in the agricultural sector is accelerating at an alarming rate and many are alarmed at today's farming practices. The Land Girls carried out much of their work by hand, coping with the changing weather and sometimes enduring injuries that came with the job.

Land Girls during World War 1 on a gate. (*Wikimedia*)

Some women learnt to drive for the first time as part of the WLA. (*Donated by Farmers Guardian*)

Much of the work was done by hand. (*Donated by Farmers Guardian*)

Many worked in groups. (*Donated by Farmers Guardian*)

The WLA carried out various tasks. (*Donated by Farmers Guardian*)

Many loved the outdoor life and felt pride in their work. (*Donated by Farmers Guardian*)

Hand milking. (*Donated by Farmers Guardian*)

Many sustained injuries to their hands due to the manual nature of the work . (*Donated by Farmers Guardian*)

Women's Land Army trainees enjoy a 'mite' of milk before training begins at the Northampton Institute of Agriculture in 1942. (*Wikimedia*)

Land Girls Eileen Barry (left) and Audrey Willis in 1942, preparing rat poison as part of their training at a farm in Sussex. (*Wikimedia*)

Land Army member, Vera Howson, with an axe over her shoulder between 1939 and 1945. (*Wikimedia*)

Audrey Prickett and Betty Long put bait in a trap in a haystack as part of their training at a Sussex farm. Apparently, the trap is pre-baited with unpoisoned food for three days. The rat will eat it, building its confidence and then on the fourth day, the trap is left empty meaning that the rat is hungry for the fifth day, when the trap is poisoned. (*Wikimedia*)

Cambridgeshire, England, 1942. May Edwards drives past a ditcher crane, towing a trailer full of other members of the Land Army with a pile of roots and reeds they have removed from the newly reclaimed fen land. (*Wikimedia*)

May Edwards driving the tractor. (*Wikimedia*)

Here are Land Girls Ivy Reid, Alice Crook, Joy Godsall and a colleague digging an old bog oak out of a piece of reclaimed fen land in Cambridgeshire in 1942. (*Wikimedia*)

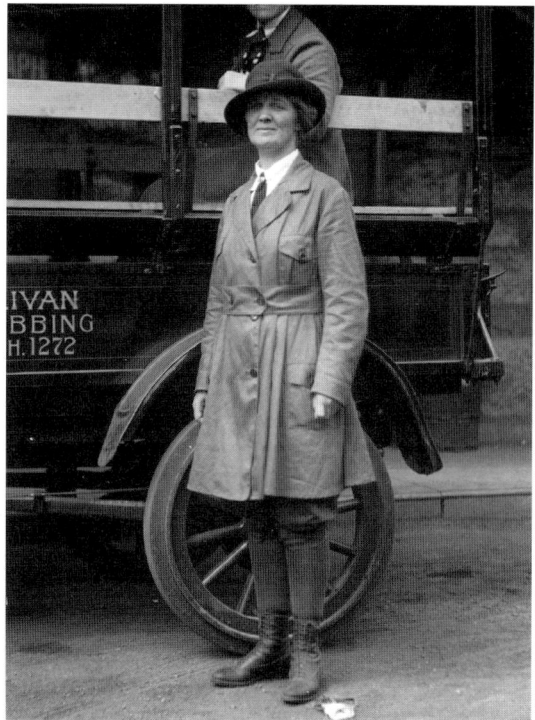

This is an American Land Girl, Miss Zela Knowlton in World War 1, at Wellesley College, Massachusetts. The course included agriculture, cooking and hygiene. (*Wikimedia*)

These are Land Army girls in Victoria, Australia, employed at the Drouin flax mill. The girls get 3 pound ten shillings a week, which is about 75 percent of the wage men were paid for the same work. (*Wikimedia*)

WLA members cleaning mangelwurzels for cattle fodder at a training camp, in Cannington, Somerset, England, 1940. (*Wikimedia*)

Farmer Tuppin in
Sussex, 1942, leading
a team of Land Girls
into a battle against rats.
(*Wikimedia*)

Girl's brussel sprout picking as part of their training at Cannington Farm, Somerset in 1940. (*Wikimedia*)

A Woman in Time

Whether consciously or not, for me the Land Girls were true equality seekers. In fact, all women who did their bit, no matter how small, played a part in changing the narrative about a woman's capability.

The WLA especially received a great deal of negativity regarding their ability to cope with farm work, despite their competency and achievements during the First World War. Even Lady Denman, D.B.E, Honorary Director of the WLA, wrote:

> Farmers' memories are short, and in spite of the good work done on the land by women during the last war, the Land Army has had to encounter much prejudice against the employment of women's labour. This prejudice has now almost everywhere been overcome through the really magnificent service given by the first few thousand employed volunteers who worked through the bitter winter of 1939 under conditions of great difficulty and loneliness and have stuck to their jobs ever since. To these volunteers and the many others with the same fine spirit now working in the Land Army the country owes a great deal.

In 1915 the feeling of discontent at this lack of appreciation was rife and women marched through the streets of London, knowing their contribution was vital in the war effort, stating: 'The situation is serious. Women must help to save it.'

Olivia Smith, public historian, says: 'This shows that even if men did not like it, women were not going to let that stop them. It is exemplary of the fact that women were not initially welcomed, and the popular memory of the First World War is that women worked in male dominated industries.'

In the years before 1939 women were essentially keepers of the home and men were viewed as the breadwinners, but that shift of power and the need for farm workers planted the seeds for feminism to grow again after a period of female oppression. But how much truly changed post-war?

Although war created the need for women workers, it was not seen as a long-term option for females to continue working in industries they were not welcome in. Olivia Smith says:

> The unions, and many individual male workers, saw the employment of women in areas that had previously been the preserve of men as a threat to their status and pay, and rather than campaigning for pay and training to match that of men. They urged dilution, lower rates of pay and temporary contracts to ensure work and pay rates would be in place for men when they returned from war.
>
> As the numbers of women registered as unemployed soared during the post-war slump, the British Government introduced regulations that denied unemployment benefits to any woman who turned down work in domestic service. Support was lacking for those who did not want to return to their previous roles. The Restoration of Pre-War Practices Act, 1918, gave employers up to two months to return to pre-war practices and required roles to be then maintained for a year.

After the Second World War, despite the fact that the female workforce had now proved themselves twice over, workplace security was still practically non-existent. The removal of women from their roles at the end of the war was guaranteed under The Restoration of Pre-war Trade Practices Act of 1942. These women were defined as temporary, perhaps second-class, and though it was right that men who returned home from war should find employment after such sacrifice, women surely should have also been given the opportunity of employment.

Olivia Smith says:

> Essentially wartime replacement was seen as temporary and women tended to return to their old occupations and more often to marriage and home life.
>
> Within the space of 30 years, two generations of women were given the opportunity to show what they could do when it was really

needed. The opportunities that were given to women in industry, public services and military service would not have been there if the wars did not happen.

In hindsight, we know how valuable those contributions were and I would like to think the contemporaries were aware of the capability women demonstrated throughout those years. The First World War was the trial run – can women do this? So, when the Second World War came around, it was a given that women could step up and do their bit.

Since the Representation of the Peoples Act 1918, I think we have come on leaps and bounds in terms of women's equality, but we still have a long way to go. From my own experience, I have grown up with the belief that as a woman I can achieve anything, and that my gender will not hinder my doing so. That thought alone is the epitome of how far we have come. Now, women prove they can be mothers and caregivers whilst paving a career in whatever they want. The freedom we now have compared to a century ago is also liberating. I will always be thankful to the women before me, as I would not be in the fortunate position that I am in now without them.

Even the Women's Land Army uniform caused a stir. Never before was it the norm to witness a woman wearing trousers; to see a woman cut such a masculine figure was cause for discussion among some. As a Land Girl you were required to wear breeches – perhaps the most identifiable Land Girl garment – a green jersey, a hat (which resembled a Stetson and apparently caused much controversy over the way it was worn), a shirt, a pair of brogues and long socks designed to stop their feet getting wet.

I have spoken to many members who said that their uniform gave them a sense of pride and strength, but more practically, an ease of movement to work in. My own grandmother particularly liked hers, recalling how smart it made her appear with its 'nipped in waist.'

In the post-war period, after years of being called upon to help the nation and contribute to the war effort, some women found a new sense of freedom. Their former positions had given them independence and confidence and there was no going back from this. For some women, farming became a passion, and my own grandmother spent the rest of her days in the industry after marrying my grandad, Jim. Equally as many,

Gladys Monks was born in Nottingham in 1923, and joined the WLA towards the end of the Second World War. She continued in the WLA until 1947. She was stationed at Toot Hill in Bingham, and her family said she relished the tasks given to her, whether it be mucking out, feeding, or getting crops in. She particularly loved the harvest, threshing being one of her favourite things, and would always volunteer to be the one 'on top of the drum'. She met her future husband, Frank, on one of the farms, Millingtons at Orston Grange near Bottesford, and they married in 1948. She told her family that she formed many lifelong friendships, and always said the Land Army years were some of the best of her life.

though, found solace back in the home after so long working to sustain Britain as well as having to simultaneously look after their families. Tired and worn out from the war years, to raise a family in peace was enough.

Choices were still not free to make, however, with certain expectations of women still upheld. An example of such is Beryl Tacon, whose daughter, Christine Tacon, believes her own mother probably suffered from the impacts of such presumptions about a woman's place. She says:

My mother was born in 1928, the daughter of a milliner and a grocer and her brother, who was eight years older than her, went to work on a farm. She decided she wanted to work in farming too, but as she was also academic, she decided to go to university. She got into Sutton Bonington, Nottinghamshire, but there were no places

Beryl Tacon in uniform.

left as all the service men were coming back and she was told to go and join the Land Army for two years and consider going to university afterwards. I believe she then went to Writtle College for some further training before she joined the National Advisory Service, advising farmers on how to increase milk yields when the country was short of food. She had to give up her civil service career, however, when she got married in 1957. I think she resented that so much that it affected her with depression for much of her life.

Payment and Care

As Meriel Talbot had already explained, payment was one of the main concerns for the Land Girls. Unlike other women who were in service and paid by the government, it fell to the employer of the Land Girls to provide payment. After speaking to former members, pay varied depending on circumstance and was highly dependent on the farmer who paid them.

Lady Denman campaigned for a minimum wage of 28 shillings per week (£1.40), and from 1 June 1939 weekly wages were set. However, it was still 10 shillings less than the average farm wage at that time, and for most women half their wages were taken for accommodation and food. From 1 March 1941 Land Girls billeted off the farm were paid 32 shillings (£1.60) for a 48-hour week, and Land Girls billeted on-farm were paid 16 shillings (80p), plus overtime pay.

Women in the Land Army were paid less than their male counterparts since they were considered not to be as able. Right from the start there was no question of equal pay. It was Vita Sackville-West who said: 'Agriculture is one of those professions in which a man is fully justified in receiving the high wage. He gives better value for his time and money. I think most farmers would agree that the ratio would work out at three women equalling two men.' Perhaps this underpayment was due to the constraints of wartime, but it does pose the question, were these women paid less simply because they were women?

It is further interesting to find that while other members of the women's forces were under constant medical supervision, the Land Girls were certainly not. Unlike women who enrolled in other wartime services, they were expected to register with the local doctor, as the government passed responsibility to those who employed them, leaving it to the farming families to decide whether a worker needed healthcare or not. They were even told to insure themselves should they sustain an injury. It seems incredible to us

Enjoying a quiet spot on a bench under the trees in the garden of the rest break house in Torquay. (left to right) Mrs Eivemark (the forewoman of a WLA hostel), Miss Mary Pakes, Miss Ann Royne (WLA gang work forewoman) and Mrs Joan Hart (timber corps crane driver). Mrs Eivemark and Miss Pakes are chatting whilst Miss Royne and Miss Hart are reading a book together. (*Wikimedia*)

Land Girls at a rest house in Devon. (*Wikimedia*)

today that the Land Girls were left to fend for themselves in what has been proven to be one of the most dangerous industries to work.

It was interesting to receive information about Nora Wright, who desperately wanted to be a Land Girl, but was unfortunately too young. Undeterred, she signed up to work in the hostels, hoping that this would lead her to one day becoming a fully-fledged member. Nora was only 14-years-old at the time – they called her 'little Nora' – but she relished in her duties working for the Cheshire War Agricultural Committee, cooking, cleaning and maintaining the hostels. She wrote a very detailed account of her tasks – most of which she loved, some of which, involving the care of the women in the WLA, came as a surprise.

She wrote:

> "A doctor would come and lecture on venereal disease including Gonorreah and Syphilis – an eye opening but we had to know about the facts of life. Also hair care and hygeine – lice and nits.
>
> "The matron and the duty orderly – that was me – did head inspection one Friday each month – it was a hell of a job but it had to be done. In one instance about twenty two girls had to be treated for very bad cases of lice and it was my job to go to the chemist for very strong oil and cotton wool. It was very embrassaing for me and I remember saying to the chemist 'it's not for me, it's for the matron at the Land Army hostel.' I was glad to get out of the shop.
>
> "That night all those poor girls were treated with the oil. Talk about turban dresses for Land Girls, it was no laughing matter at the time.
>
> "Some of the girls actually wore turbans when working on the farms – this was for safety purposes because long hair would get in the way of the machinery."

The majority of women I have spoken to, however, believed that it was enough for them to know they were helping with the war effort, even in the smallest way. Lady Denman did lobby continuously for her girls, pushing the Ministry of Agriculture to increase the Women's Land Army's pitiful budget, and from 1944 selected Land Girls were sometimes sent to Rest Break Houses when circumstances called for it, such as long illness or a long stint in service.

The Women

Not all the stories in this book are from women I have met myself. But of those whom I have had the pleasure of speaking to, each has presented with me with an outlook on life that is so evocative of the war generation: spirit, hope, will, and a fighting nature to do what is best regardless of personal cost.

My first interview was with Jean Bindoff, and I can remember thinking that she was everything I expected a Land Girl to be. She was feisty and immediately relatable. Her stories of attending local dances with thousands of RAF soldiers, her gripes with other women in her hostel and her remarkable zest for life brought up in me memories of my own grandmother, which happened more often than not when speaking of the lives these women led.

Some were, at first, hesitant to talk, perhaps for fear of judgement. Mary Harris spoke of being sent to a punishment hostel for arriving back late on the train, yet not once did she express resentment. I think those who joined the Land Army and stuck it out understood what it truly meant; doing the job, doing it well, and, if they broke the rules, they took the repercussions.

There were also stories about relationships with German officers and prisoners of war, but still, to this day, these women felt they could not tell such tales, perhaps still plagued by guilt or fear. Or it could be that they feel it would be pointless to replay events from the past that cannot be changed, or to open old wounds?

* * *

Most of the women I spoke to were remarkably nonchalant about the lack of acknowledgement and post-war payments. The words of one former Land Girl stick in my mind. At the end of our interview, she took my hand and said, 'nobody recognised us'. I felt, in that moment, both powerless and determined to put things right: powerless because we are probably entering an era where we will lose these women, determined because maybe I can be part of change.

Perhaps I can help to shape the women of today and those of tomorrow by saying we, as females, can only move forwards positively by seeking answers from the past. The Women's Land Army did an incredible amount of work that equalled that of a man, but after the war the nation slipped back into its former gender roles and the chance to change societal hierarchies is there once again for the taking.

Sometimes I was told about their overwhelming feelings of loneliness. There were a few who confessed to being made to feel unwelcome by their farming families. Some were not even allowed to eat with their

Me and Jean Bindoff.

Me and Mary Harris.

hosts at the dinner table, and their evenings were spent alone in their rooms either writing or indulging in hobbies such as crocheting.

But for every time I felt sadness, there were more occasions where I felt nothing but happiness. On hearing how Sylvia Harper organised a reunion for all her former Land Army members, it made me realise just how much these women valued each other and their time together. Even their matron attended the gathering, and although now blind, could recognise her ladies' voices, recalling fondly – through tears – how she could remember all the things the girls got up to under her care.

Sylvia recalled how some wore their uniforms for the reunion, meeting each other's children and grandchildren, and joining together once again over thirty years after becoming a land girl as if no time had passed. That is true friendship; the unbreakable bond so many of these women speak of.

Sylvia helped to organise Land Girl reunions.

Many of these women possessed the knack of storytelling which only comes from people who have lived an age, and their effervescent tales of Saturday night dances and romances, of weaving their way home from the village hall in the dead of night on the backs of motorcycles, are purely the actions of young teenage women enjoying their youth, and no more than expected when no one had a clue what the future held.

For those who sent me stories written by the women sadly not with us, I cannot express my gratitude enough. Without them I could not have done this. I also must say that in the process of writing we have said goodbye to some of those featured in the book, and I can only hope that I have done some good in capturing their stories for all.

There were also stories that came through in snippets, or tales passed over generations. One in particular is from award-winning author Peter Lion who shared the following:

During the war, Wales was used for overseas training for American troops, especially prior to the D-Day invasion. In October of 1943, the 28th Infantry Division arrived in Wales for such training. More than any other division or group of soldiers, the members of the 28th were embraced by the people of Wales. The 28th ID, prior to the war, was the Pennsylvania National Guard. Pennsylvania, especially the western half of the state, was (and in some places still is) "mining country". There, iron ore for making steel was what was mined. It is no surprise that when people from Wales emigrated to the US in search of a better life, their mining skills were in demand in this area. Hence, when the 28th found itself in Wales for training, some of the soldiers in the division had distant relatives still living there. So, the people in Wales, while not entirely thrilled with having to share their homes and their towns with the Yanks, were most accommodating to the soldiers of the 28th, who would remain in Wales for the next seven months.

One of the towns where these soldiers were settled was St. Clears, mostly members of the 28th Infantry Division's 28th Cavalry Reconnaissance Troop. In fact, Pen-y-Coed mansion was their headquarters and I believe it is a hospital/rehab facility of some type now. Well, while in St. Clears, as you can imagine during the course of the next seven months, the soldiers became quite friendly with the local population, with many a night spent hoisting pints at the Black Lion Pub, a favourite haunt. It was during one of those nights that a young soldier named Dan Garbo from the Recon Troop met 18-year-old land girl Emma Friar. Emma, like many land girls, had been living in London when war broke out, and was encouraged by her family to join the Women's Land Army as a way of getting her out of harm's way. In doing so she was relocated to the farm-rich lands surrounding St. Clears.

The two fell in love and spent as much time together as possible, knowing that the clock was always ticking. In May of 1944, just ahead of the invasion […] the 28th was ordered east to "ready positions". Before leaving, as I am sure was many a soldiers' promise, Dan pledged that if he survived the war he would come back to Emma.

As fate would have it, despite the odds and battles and close calls, Dan did survive the war and made good on his pledge. He returned to St. Clears and indeed found Emma. The two were married at St. Mary's Church and then moved to Dan's home in a suburb of Chicago to start a family and their lives together. Tragically, a year later, Emma died giving birth to the couple's only child, a daughter. Unable to cope with the loss of his beloved Emma and the prospect of raising a child on his own, Dan gave the girl up for adoption. Dan died in 1982 at the age 63.

I was also overwhelmed to hear stories from those who emigrated after the war, either in search of a better life or through marriage. Coincidentally, I had a conversation with the daughter of a Land Girl who originated from Liverpool, just like my grandma, and went on to be stationed just miles down the road from her. Whether they ever met we shall never know, but the stories that bind us from across the globe are what link us all in some way, from generation to generation.

For those I spoke to personally, I always asked them the same question: would they do it all again if they had the choice to? And I can unequivocally say that every single one said 'yes'. No hesitation, no consideration. For the friendships they made, for the experience it gave them, for the love they found, all hold their memories of the time in the Women's Land Army close their hearts.

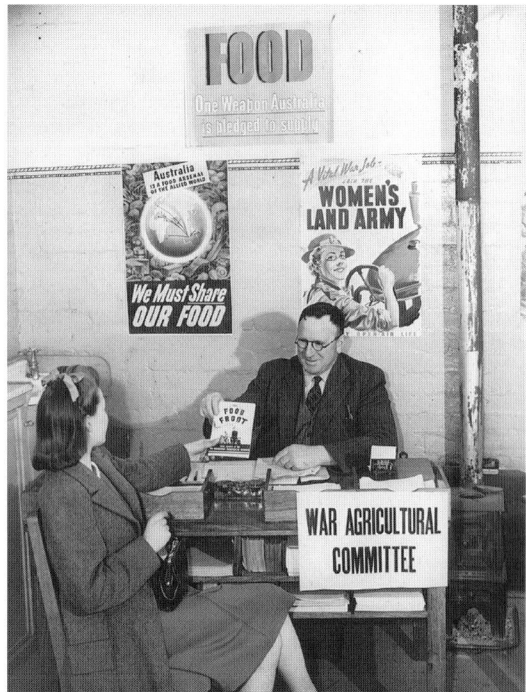

The Australian Women's Land Army was also created in World War Two. Here is Arthur Holmes for the War Agricultural Committee enrolling Helen Dixon in Drouin, Victoria. (*Wikimedia*)

Land Girls in Fenland in Cambridgeshire. (*Wikimedia*)

Land Girls placing chickens into cages at Charing Cross underground station in London during 1942. (*Wikimedia*)

Land Girls in
West Sussex in
1944. (*Wikimedia*)

Land Girl milking
during World War
One. (*Wikimedia*)

Land Girl Iris Joyce
with other members
in a railway carriage.
(*Wikimedia*)

Land Girl holding a chicken in 1944. (*Wikimedia*)

Rest and relaxation house for WLA members in Devon 1944. (*Wikimedia*)

Land Girl in an Essex village in 1941. (*Wikimedia*)

Land Girls were expected to look after poultry. (*Wikimedia*)

'Ten little Land Girls'

Jean Moncrieff, Secretary, WLA Benevolent Fund

Ten little Land Girls went to feed the swine,
One said "oh, what a boar!" and then there were nine.
Nine little Land Girls learned to incubate,
One was no chicken, and then there were eight.
Eight little Land Girls milking down in Devon,
One kicked the bucket, and then there were seven.
Seven little Land Girls piling up the ricks,
One went hay-wire, and then there were six.
Six little Land Girls a tractor learned to drive,
The farmer ploughed one, and then there were five.
Five little Land Girls had never stripped before,
One did a tease act, and then there were four.
Four little Land Girls, tried to fell a tree,
One fell for the forester, and then there were three.
Three little Land Girls to geese could not say "boo,"
One went to Uganda, and then there were two.
One little Land Girl when her work was done,
Turned up the "bridle" path, and then there was none.

My Grandma, Vera May Whyte Ashworth (née Flemming)

Honestly? My Grandma was a beauty. She had smooth, porcelain skin as pale as fresh milk. The auburn hair that once fell around her perfectly formed cheekbones burned brightly, much like her character, I guess.

Born Vera May Whyte Flemming on 26 April 1926, my grandma was a fiery Liverpudlian and even after living in Lancashire for most of her life, every now and then her accent, that slight twang, would appear mid-sentence.

She received her call-up papers for the Women's Land Army in 1944, aged eighteen, having just finished her apprenticeship in fashion. She was sent to Somerset to begin her journey as a Land Girl.

My grandma, Vera May Whyte Ashworth.

She was not totally unaware of the workings of the countryside, often reminiscing of her much-loved family trips to Ireland, but to go from the bustle of Liverpool to Low Moor, the quiet, picture-perfect village where I have found myself back living, was surely a shock. The sound of the countryside still fills the air, and we are still woken by local donkeys braying and morning bird song.

I asked her once if she resented the fact that she never got to work in the fashion industry, the chance pulled from right under her like so many other wartime women.

I know she was stylish; I could just tell. She had an eye for design and material and always read the style pages in the Sunday magazines, discussing the latest trends with me, or briskly unleashing her opinion about what 'girls these days wore'.

Would she have led a life in fashion? One can never say, but these women were needed regardless of personal ambition or status, and grandma, shall we say, was not the sentimental type; she held no grudges or bitterness, instead pondering perhaps that had she entered the fashion industry her life may not have been as 'colourful'. And of course, I would not exist.

The fresh air and the outdoor life suited her well and it was how she met my grandad, James – or Jim as everyone called him – a twist of fate that led her to spend the rest of her days as a dairy farmer (which was also true of many other former WLA members).

Low Moor farm covered about 57 acres, running a mix of Holsteins, Friesians, Jerseys and Albions, bought by my great grandad, James. Interestingly, it was originally owned by the Garnett family who owned the infamous Low Moor textile mill. My grandad began a milk round from the farm, which was then taken over by my dad and his brothers in the 1970s.

It is funny how writing her story makes me feel connected to my home in Lancashire. I walk past the farmhouse most days, with its cherry blossom tree that flourishes each year and brings our small village to life, reminding me that she is still around.

Grandma was well known in our village for her sharp tongue and naughty wit, but her bark was worse than her bite. I do wonder whether her stint in the Land Army made her believe she always had to be a tough cookie.

Old pictures of Low Moor Farm.

There were countless conversations in which she would recall outshining any man working on the farm with her, suggesting that she had to strive to prove her worth. The farm was also frequented by Italian prisoners of war, most of whom she found quite pleasant.

Certain stories stick with me, though, from the snapshots she gave me of her time in the WLA, and it saddens me that I never took pen to paper more when she was living. But the following stands out, from one of the very first articles I wrote on the Land Army:

We were out threshing kale in the middle of a freezing day in November. My hands were all blistered but the girl working next to me started to cry and sat down right where she stood.

She said she could not do it anymore, so I just took my own gloves and coat off and gave them to her.

I actually enjoyed it and found myself quite toasty once I had finished.

It is these moments which, to me, say everything that needs to be said, not just about my own grandma, but about the silent promise these women seemed to make to each other. It brings to life the many anecdotes of friendships formed between these women, and the support they gave to each other.

She also told of how scared she had been after riding her bicycle too fast around the winding Somerset lanes, carting a tray of milk on the front of her bike. Turning too sharply, her balance went and along with it the milk. But her first thoughts were of the farmer and how angry he was going to be when he found out how she had spilled the milk. I could not imagine her being scared of anyone, I said.

Then there was the time she and some other Land Girls managed to find a bag of cigarettes, charmed no doubt out of the hands of local American soldiers. Once back at their hostel, they had to creep in through a window and hide their stash from the warden. They hid them in a water tank and went back to find there had been a hole in the bag and their cigarettes were wet and ruined.

There was also her rather bumpy introduction to life in the Land Army. On her first night she had been allocated the top bunk in a cold barn where the girls slept. Grandma had forgotten where she was, rolled over and fell with thump on to the floor!

When reading back through all these stories, you can feel the kind of innocence that only young people have. And that is what many of these women were – young and carefree, but bound by duty and making the best of their situation.

Grandma's life turned out very differently to what she could ever have imagined when just eighteen, and to sit and look back over ninety years of her life must have been a strange conversation to have. Could she have made it in fashion? Was it a cruel twist of events? Whatever it was, I am just so blessed that she was my grandma and I want her to know that I am so proud of what she did. And if there is something I would like to live by, it is her parting statement from that very first interview: 'I have always made the very best of situations.'

My grandparents on their wedding day.

This collection of images was kindly shared with me by Kathy Mills, whose grandparent's, John and Elizabeth Sephton, were tenant farmers at Winacre Farm in Lancashire. With potatoes to pick, John applied to the Women's Land Army after receiving a letter from the Agricultural Labour Board. 14 Land Girls were billeted there, and their jobs included digging potatoes, weighing and bagging. This provides a good insight into what like as a Land Girl in Lancashire might have been like. There are also various newspaper clippings kept by the family, some of which show John's great appreciation for his workforce.

Women's Land Army –
1941 World War II
at Winacre Farm

John and Elizabeth Sephton welcomed a large number of Land Girls on to their farm in Lancashire, and they did so with open arms.

The Land Girls

The couple were fondly thought of by all the women who worked on their farm.

It is 1941 and 60 acres of potatoes are ready to be picked at Winacre Farm

- Traditionally the potatoes would be picked with the aid of seasonal travelling Irishmen, but no longer available beacuse of the war.
- Prompted by a letter received from the Agricultural Labour Board, John Sephton applied to the Women's Land Army for potato pickers.
- The Land Army secretary offered to provide 14 girls to stay at the farm provided each could have a single bed. John and Elizabeth combed the neighbourhood for beds and the girls duly arrived.
- The girls were from various backgrounds: office girls, shop workers, kennel maid and even a lady's maid. Some were straight from college.

The first 14 Land Army girls to arrive at Winacre, pictured with John and Elizabeth (centre) and Women's Land Army representatives each side.

Dinner with the girls at Winacre.

Many of the girls had boyfriends in the Forces, and much of their free time was spent writing letters.

Land Girls working the land.

The girls were welcomed and were involved in activities off the farm too.

Some of the Land Girls at Winacre.

Relationships and friendships were made.

It was very manual and hands on work.

The girls collectively got the job done.

Girls out in the countryside.

Soldiers visiting.

The working day was 8am until 12pm and 1pm until 5.30pm. Outside of that the time is their own.

The new power digger in use.

Lifting the
spuds into
baskets.

Potatoes were brought in by hand.

It could be dirty work gathering potatoes.

Weighing and bagging.

All together for a group picture.

Out in the fields in their farm uniform.

Working hard to pick the potatoes by hand.

The women at Winacre enjoyed their time in the WLA.

Most women had to learn on the job.

Sorting the potatoes.

Storing the potatoes in a clamp.

Plenty of time for a little leisure. Wednesday night was usually a trip into town.

The girls having dinner with Tom and Betty, the Sephton's children.

John gives the girls a lesson in billiards.

The girls

An iconic guard of honour.

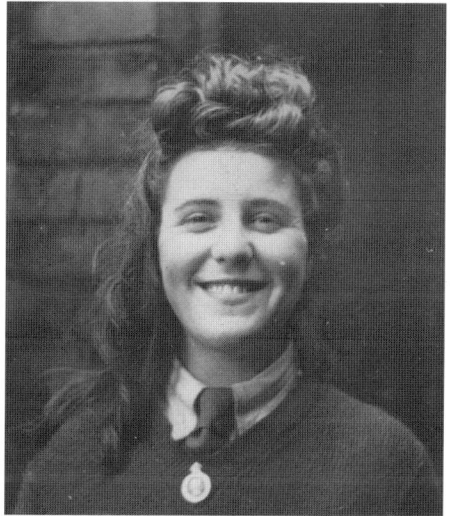

The girls 1942. Five of the 1941 girls came back with them.

Cattle at Winacre.

Working with pigs.

They were long and labour intense days on the farm.

PENWORTHAM

The wedding took place on Friday of last week of Miss Jessie Mavis Knight, youngest daughter of Mr. and Mrs. H. Knight, of 52, Shaftesbury-avenue, Penwortham, and Mr. Peter Lindsay Martin, youngest son of Mr. and Mrs. H. Martin, of Brighton Sussex. The service was conducted by the Rev. Jas. C. H. H. Fordham, of Holy Trinity Church, Blackpool. The bride is a member of the Women's Land Army and the bridegroom is serving with the R.A.F. The bride, who was given away by her father, wore a gown of white lace, with wreath and veil, and carried a shower bouquet of pink carnations. Her bridesmaid, a sister of the bridegroom, was dressed in pink satin with a Victorian posy of pink carnations. The best man was Mr. T. Heywood, friend of the bride and bridegroom. After the ceremony a reception was held at the bride's home. Among the gifts was the wedding cake, given by Mr. and Mrs. Sephton, employers of the bride.

One of the girls marries her RAF boyfriend – the cake was given by John and Elizabeth.

The girls expressed their gratitude to John and Elizabeth.

The potatoes are all in and the girls have finished the job, so a trip to the theatre is in order.

- As thanks for a job well done John takes the party to the Garrick Theatre along with his wife and children.
- Theatregoers were used to seeing service uniforms of khaki, navy and air force blue but the girls caused a sensation to their beholders in their smart green jerseys, whipcord breeches and jaunty hats. The event was widely reported in the press.
- Amongst the entertainers were the famous Doris and Elsie Waters who presented the party with their signed photograph.
- The girls showed their appreciation by presenting John with a silver cigarette case, and Elizabeth with a dainty handbag.

FARM GIRLS CAUSE THEATRE SENSATION

LEAVE FIELDS TO SEE SOUTHPORT SHOW

There was a sensation at the Garrick Theatre on Wednesday night.

Southport is used to uniforms, quite blasé in fact about khaki, navy and Air Force blue, ribbons and stars are to be seen everywhere, and the ring of the Service boot is a familiar sound. All those were present at the Garrick, plus another contingent, in smart green jerseys, whipcord breeches and jaunty hats.

To quote Mr. Sephton, 'I asked for a box of tricks and I got a box of bricks."

Prompted by a letter received from the Agricultural Labour Bureau at Hutton, suggesting the type of labour available, the farmer applied recently to the Women's Land Army sub-branch at Preston for potato pickers.

With the result that fourteen stalwart lasses descended upon Winacre.

Blondes and brunettes were well mixed; there was a good splinkling of Scottish and Irish among them, some had been used to office work, others had been in shops, one had been a ladies' maid, another a kennel maid, but there have been no differences of opinion and no squabbling while at the farm.

WEARERS O' THE GREEN

Beholders at the Garrick metaphorically rubbed their eyes as they admired.

Wearers of the green were a party of "landgirls," members of the Women's Land Army, and they were having a night out as a reward for being good girls and good workers.

They had been potato picking for the last three weeks at Winacre Farm, Martinmere, owner Mr. John Sephton, whose guests they were at the theatre.

Mr. Sephton told a "Southport Guardian" woman reporter that he was more than satisfied with the way the girls have "stuck in" on the job. This is the first time he has employed woman labour on Winacre Farm, and he's so pleased he'll do it again.

The majority have boy friends in

AFTER THE POTATOES

This year Mr. Sephton has turned over to a power digger, and the girls work in sections after the machine, each with a basket which will hold about 30 lbs. of potatoes, tipped into hampers when full. Mrs. John Sephton and Mrs. Nather

WHERE ... AND

TWELVE months ago I went to the Churchtown farm of Mr. J. Sephton, a well-known potato grower, pig breeder, and horse breeder, to see about 14 Land Girls working at once on his farm. Land Girls were then by no means as popular as they are to-day with farmers, and Mr. Sephton was regarded as something of a pioneer in having so many girls in his employ.

But the real proof of the utility of girls such as these lies not simply in their hiring for one harvest. Mr. Sephton declared himself well satisfied with their work last year, but I felt that the real test would be to see if he was relying upon girls again this year to help him with the harvesting.

So on Monday I turned up at his farm quite unexpectedly to see what was happening. I strolled out to the potato field which presented a scene of great activity, and there I found Mr. Sephton superintending the work of another 14 Land Girls who have replaced those who were hired last season.

By his action in hiring Land Girls once again, Mr. Sephton has shown his appreciation of their services in a manner he could not have indicated by words. No farmer is willing to hire unproductive labour; by engaging 14 Land Girls again, Mr. Sephton has shown conclusively that he believes them adequately fitted for the job and is, indeed, full of praise for the work they do.

He has an advantage in that he can accommodate them all at the farm and he points out that the great advantage at the potato lifting season is that they are on the spot each morning and he knows just how much labour he can count upon from day to day. This is far more satisfactory than relying upon casual labour.

The girls work hard, too, shifting a good 20 tons of potatoes a day, which is not bad going, and does not allow for any shirking. At this farm the welfare of the girls is well looked after and they repay the kindness shown them in their strict devotion to their work.

A Good Crop

When I called the girls were busy picking King Edwards, which have yielded amazingly well on this land, which was originally the bed of Martin Mere. I understand from Mr. Sephton that the average is close on ten tons to the ...

grand sow, and which I saw Mr. Sephton buy at the last Whittingham sale. I was glad to know that Mr. Sephton is surmounting the rationing difficulties in the most practical way. He has cut down the number of pigs kept very extensively, but is keeping pigs of the best strains and families, he can procure. Quality rather than quantity is necessary in these days of feeding-stuff shortage.

At Winacre

On my way back from Southport on Monday I took the opportunity to call upon Mr. Sephton, at Winacre Farm, near Churchtown. Mr. Sephton is one of the latest recruits to the ranks of pedigree breeders and I was anxious to how he was progressing.

From what I saw of the stock boar, a Whittingham bred youngster, descended from the famous Wall Majestic 59th, and from some of the sows which represent many of the famous strains of Large Whites, including a goodly selection from the lately dispersed Walton herd, it looks as though Mr. Sephton will have a well-established herd in another two or three years. He is certainly convinced that there will be a big trade for pedigree pigs after the war.

Danish Piggery

Incidentally, there appears on this page a photograph of his Danish piggery, which was built by himself and a joiner to his own specifications. There is no lack of room for the building, which is of wood on a low wall of concrete and bricks, measuring 120 feet by 30 feet has 24 pens each measuring 10 feet by eight feet.

A feature is the commodious dung passage and the ample centre gangway with the overhead trolley system of feeding, which makes the work much lighter than it would otherwise be.

The ventilation has been carefully studied, and includes a system of low wall ventilation, side windows and raised apex windows on the louvre principle.

Mr. Sephton is finding it possible to rear a considerable number of stores, chiefly crossed from his Large White and Essex breeds. The feeding problem is eased by

IMPORTANT SALE AT WINACRE FARM, MOSS LANE, CHURCHTOWN, SOUTHPORT (2½ miles from Churchtown or Queens Railway Station).

E. G. ROTHERSALL & SONS, LTD., are favoured with instructions from Mr. JOHN SEPHTON (leaving the district) to SELL by AUCTION, on THURSDAY NEXT, January 14th, the VALUABLE HORSES, PIGS, MACHINERY, Etc., viz.:

5 HORSES: 1, Brown Gelding, rising 5; 15-2hds.; 2, Black Gelding, rising 4, 16-2hds.; 3, Bay Gelding, rising 4, 16-2hds.; 4, Bay Gelding, rising 4, 16-2hds.; 5, Bay Van Mare, 7yrs., 15hds. The above are very active, with good legs and feet, and well-known good workers and quiet.

203 PIGS: Four Young Essex Sows, due about sale and March; two Essex Sows, newly served; one Essex Sow and 10 followers; one Welsh Sow, newly served; three Young L.W. Boars, ready for service; 132 Strong Store Pigs, L.W. and Essex cross, 60 Speaners.

FARM IMPLEMENTS & MACHINERY, chiefly in excellent condition, includes: Fordson Tractor (1946) on spade lugs; International F12 Tractor with Row Crop attachment and power mower; Oliver No. 2A Two-furrow Tractor Plough, Two-row Ridger, Artificial Manure Distributor, Elevator Type Potato Digger, by Oliver; Martin 12-disc Tractor Cultivator, International 15-spout Corn Drill, Wallace Manure Distributor, Tandem Disc Harrows, by Deering; Cooch Potato Riddle, for power; Albion Potato Planter, iron Land Roller, R.W. & T.C.F. Ploughs, 2-drill Harrows, two sets Diamond Harrows, Scarifier, Top Harrow, R.T. Low Manure Cart, Stiff Cart with H.G., B.T. Flat Cart with h.g. and side-boards; Four-wheel Implement Bogie; two Spring Lorries, 14 and 15cwt., with side-boards, by Hardman and Hill Rose; Massey-Harris 7ft. Self-Binder, with tractor attachment; ditto by Deering, for power; Roberts Hay Elevator, for horse or power; do., for apron; South Turner, Jarmain Side Rake, Hay Rake, Bamford Corn Grinder and Crusher, No. 20; Bentall Hay Chopper, for power; 700 Spitting Beans, Bamford 6-h.p. Stationary Engine; Upright Boiler, eft. x 5tn., insulated to 80lb., with piping complete; large Steel Tank, 6ft. 2in. x 3ain. x 38ins.; Centrifugal Sin. Pump, with 4in. piping; two 150gall. Oil Tanks, with taps; large iron Water Tank, 12½ft. x 4ft.; quantity 2in. Steel Piping, four iron Baths, Arable Spare Parts, four wood Cattle Troughs, 6ft.; large Steel Ventilator, Cabin 40 x 20 in sections, Joiner's Bench and Vice, three sets Cart Gears, two sets Leading Traces, Three Plowing Traces, and other Effects.

SURPLUS FURNITURE includes Bedroom Suite, pair Ptd. Toilets, Up. Sofa and two Easy Chairs, Up. Walnut single Chairs, Reclining Chair, Side Tables, two Feather and three Flock Beds, Coleman Petrol and Oil Lamps, Rippingill Oil Stove, Val'or Oil Stove, Small Iron Kettle, etc.

SALE at 12.15 Prompt with Implements.

On account of the numerous lots, a punctual attendance is requested.

E. G. ROTHERSALL & SONS, LTD.

The Land's the Thing!

MRS. SEPHTON, of Winacre Farm, Churchtown, says she will miss the merry voices and the sing-songs round the old organ when ten of the twelve Land Army girls employed for the potato picking season leave the farm to-morrow.

They have been with the Sephton's for nearly eight weeks now, working with the tractor-driven "digger" to harvest the 60-acre potato crop (which this year has been a "bumper one.")

Before the war Mr. Sephton employed a gang of fork-digging Irishmen for his crops, but says he finds the girls as good. "All of them stand up well to the work, and in spite of the hard weather and conditions they have had to put up with there is no grumbling or slacking, and they all get on well with us and with each other, which is the main thing."

Most of the girls were "peg pushers" in various types of offices before the war—one was a hairdresser—and none of them have ever done farm work (except, perhaps, during a brief farming holiday) before.

Irene and Frances Stevenson, of Paisley, are the two girls of the dozen who are staying on at Winacre Farm to help with the cattle, the pigs, and various other jobs about the place.

Last year Mr. Sephton had 16 land girls working for him, and all of them were fully trained. Of this year's crew five were new recruits. All the girls are volunteers.

Their hours are from 8 to 12 and from 1 to 5.30, and ... while their time is their own—spent mainly in writing letters (home and to boy-friends serving with the Forces), singing, sewing or coming into town. Wednesday is their usual "Southport night out."

Mr. and Mrs. Sephton are going to take their girls out to tea and then to the Garrick for a last night "farewell" party to-night before they leave town. All are sorry to be going, but some have hopes of returning for next year's potato harvest.

Newspaper cuttings about the farm and the Land Girls.

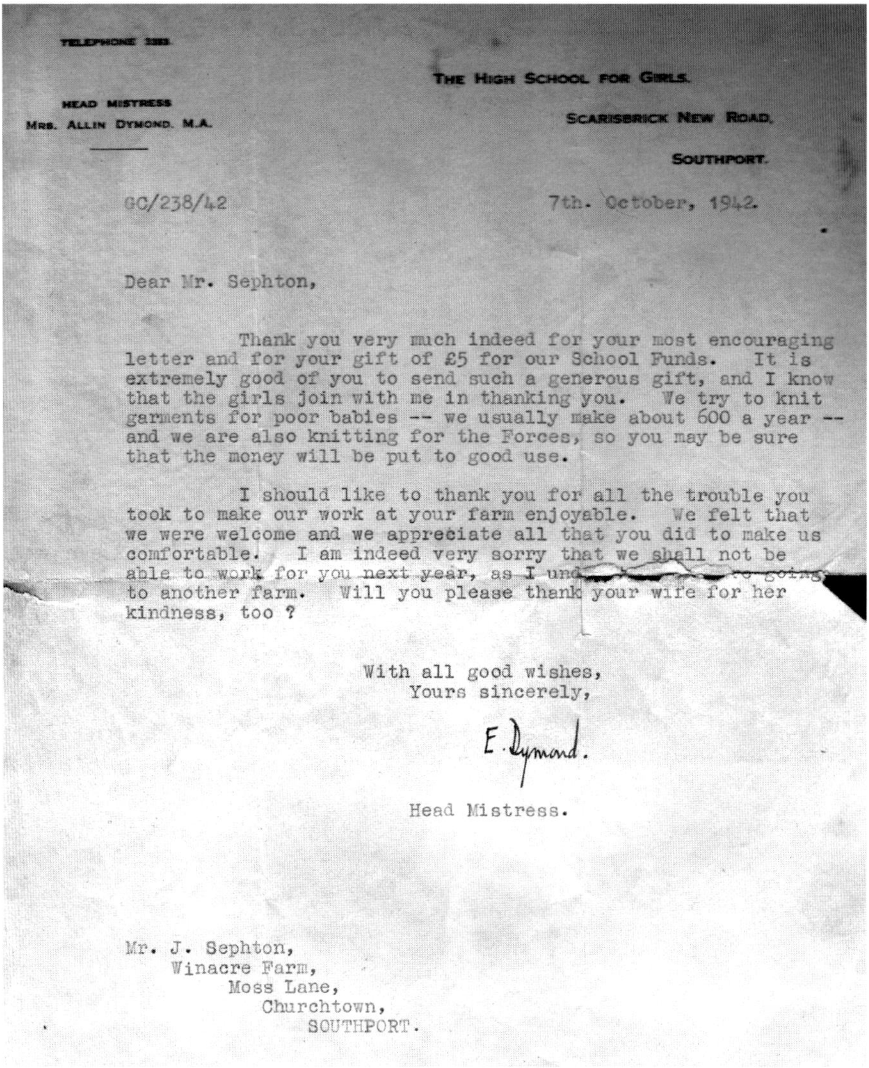

TELEPHONE 3393.

THE HIGH SCHOOL FOR GIRLS.

HEAD MISTRESS
MRS. ALLIN DYMOND. M.A.

SCARISBRICK NEW ROAD.

SOUTHPORT.

GC/238/42   7th. October, 1942.

Dear Mr. Sephton,

          Thank you very much indeed for your most encouraging
letter and for your gift of £5 for our School Funds.   It is
extremely good of you to send such a generous gift, and I know
that the girls join with me in thanking you.   We try to knit
garments for poor babies -- we usually make about 600 a year --
and we are also knitting for the Forces, so you may be sure
that the money will be put to good use.

          I should like to thank you for all the trouble you
took to make our work at your farm enjoyable.   We felt that
we were welcome and we appreciate all that you did to make us
comfortable.   I am indeed very sorry that we shall not be
able to work for you next year, as I und_____ going
to another farm.   Will you please thank your wife for her
kindness, too ?

                    With all good wishes,
                    Yours sincerely,

                         E. Dymond.

                    Head Mistress.

Mr. J. Sephton,
     Winacre Farm,
          Moss Lane,
               Churchtown,
                    SOUTHPORT.

A letter of thanks.

Land Girls at Mr. Sephton's Farm were so delighted with the arrangements made for their comfort that they presented gifts to the farmer and his wife. Included in the group are Lady Worsley-Taylor (right), president of the Lancashire Land Army, and Mrs. Robertson (left) secretary.

Winacre Farm today.

14 GIRLS 'LIFT' 60 ACRES

First Farm Job

By Daily Mail Reporter

FOURTEEN pretty girls celebrated their first big job of farm work last night in the dining-room of a Lancashire farmhouse.

They had a sausage and chip potato supper, a rollicking sing-song, and a vote of thanks to their host and hostess.

The girls, all members of the Land Army, answered an appeal for help five weeks ago.

The farmer, Mr. John Sephton, of Winacre Farm, Churchtown, Southport, had 60 acres of potatoes ready for harvesting and no one to pick them.

Offer Accepted

He was offered 14 Land Army girls.

" Where can they stay? " wired the Land Army secretary.

" With us," replied Mr. Sephton.

" Right—if they can have single beds," was the answer.

Mr. and Mrs. Sephton combed the neighbourhood. They got 14 single beds and turned rooms into dormitories. The girls arrived.

Last night they had nearly finished their big task. Most of them leave for new farm jobs this week-end.

When the back of the work had been broken Mr. and Mrs. Sephton took the girls in a party to a Southport theatre.

That was the farmer's thanks for work well done. And last night the girls showed their appreciation by presenting the farmer with a silver cigarette-case and his wife with a dainty handbag.

Mrs. Sephton told me last night: " These girls have done fine for us. They are hard workers. My husband has nothing but praise for them. As a special treat I've made them a cream pudding to-night."

Miss Greta Ellerson, who was a clerk in a Manchester office in peace-time, told me : " We've enjoyed it. It was the first job after our training for most of us. We hope all our other jobs are as pleasant as this one.

" Our ranks include a shorthand-typist, a nurse, and girls straight from college."

This year's potato crop is one of the heaviest for some years. Here is a picture taken on a Lancashire farm of Land Army girls assisting in gathering this vital crop.

More newspaper cuttings about the work of the WLA.

'The Monstrous Regiment'

by Alice Coats, Warwickshire

What hosts of women everywhere I see!
I'm sick to death of them – and they of me.
(The few remaining men are small and pale –
War lends a spurious value to the male.)
Mechanics are supplanted by their mothers;
Aunts take the place of artisans and others;
Wives sell the sago, daughters drive the van,
Even the mansion is without a man!
Females are farming who were frail before,
Matrons attending meetings by the score,
Maidens are minding multiple machines,
And virgins vending station-magazines.
Dames, hoydens, wenches, harridans and hussies,
Cram to congestion all the trams and buses;
Misses and grandmas, mistresses and nieces,
Infest bombed buildings, picking up the pieces.
Girls from the South and lassies from the North,
Sisters and sweethearts, bustle back and forth.
The newsboy and the boy who drives the plough:
Postman and milkman – all are ladies now.
Doctors and engineers – yes, even these –
Poets and politicians, all are shes.
(The very beasts that in the meadow browse
Are ewes and mares, heifers and hens and cows)
All, doubtless, worthy to a high degree;
But oh, how boring! Yes, including me.

Jean Bindoff

Born 5 July, 1926; Joined the Women's Land Army in 1946

'You know, my birthday is on July 4, so the whole of America celebrates my birthday, ha!

'I joined the Women's land Army in 1946 because I liked the idea of the countryside, of the outdoors.

'I grew up in Birmingham and when everybody else was getting evacuated, my mother would not let us leave home and there was eight of us in my family. She said if one us goes we all must go. We were bombed every night, but it was just accepted.

'I was only 18 at the time but joining up completely altered my life because suddenly, it was like, "yes, I'm free!"

Jean Bindoff with Land Girls.

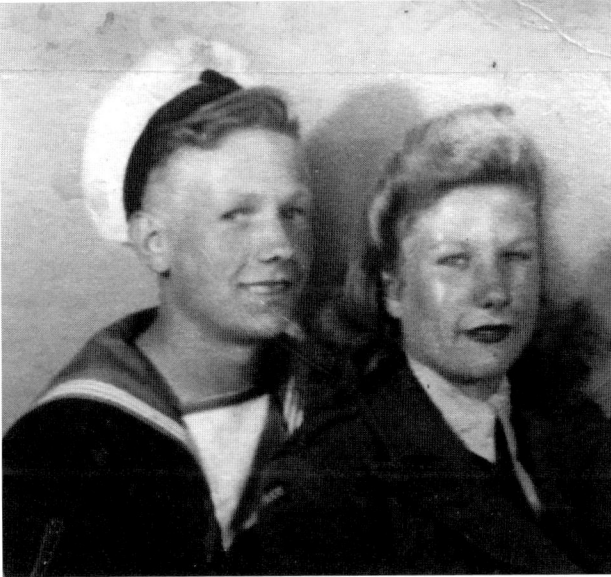

Jean Bindoff with her brother.

'There were no rules or regulations and when we were growing up, I had never been given the chance to see anything like I did in the countryside before.

'I was posted to Brill, Buckinghamshire, and I felt so independent getting the train on my own. I had to report to a group in Aylesbury, to be told where we were going and funnily enough, I found another girl called Meg who was also from Birmingham. I had never met her before though.

'We ended up being posted to the same place, and up until she passed away in 2017 I wrote to her every single Christmas. For me, it was the camaraderie that made it. That's what it was all about.

'There were not many arguments, but I do remember there was this one girl from South London, Gloria. I spoke all "Ah-la-la" at the time. You know, The Queen's English, darling!

'Gloria turned to me and said, "What the bleeding hell do you think you are doing talking like that?"

'I turned to her and told her damn straight, "Do not dare speak to me like that!" And that was it. We became friends after a while.

'We got around 30 shillings per week but believe me, they would throw us out in all weather, from the blazing sun to snow up to our knees.

'I was never actually based on a farm but in a hostel with about 38 other girls. Each morning a truck would come to pick us up and drop us wherever we were needed. I did a lot of ploughing – there is a knack to that, I am telling you. You had to do it in a certain pattern, you know.

'I remember the worst winter, too, in 1946, when the snow was halfway up the telephone poles. We were ditching and hedging with a slasher which was a length of wood with a long blade on the end. It was bloody cold, I tell you, and sometimes if it rained, I would have to get under my tractor sheet for shelter.

'But I think the hardest time was what we called double summertime, when the hours were 7am until 10pm. You would just get in to bed and before you knew it, it was time to get up again. I have always worked hard though, all my life. I do not remember having much to eat, mind you.

'There was an Irish woman in charge, and I am sure she was selling the food or eating it herself. Once, I went home and my mum said, "What are they feeding you? You are as far through as a tram ticket!" I loved it though.

'There was a dance at the village hall every Saturday evening and just up the road was a base with 23,000 men. You could not lose, could you? I had five proposals!

'I remember an encounter with my first husband, John. Me and Meg were having a shandy at the bar – that is what we drank then you see, shandy – and he was stood in the doorway.

'To his dismay I had a drink in each hand, and he said, "You're not old enough to drink!"

'I told him straight. "I am. I'm 18!" And off he went. It was a laugh!

'Overall, I think my favourite thing was driving the tractor, especially on those country roads. I was once reported for speeding on it. I was still driving up until a couple of years ago.

'I am really very proud of being a Land Girl. We say, "like birds of a feather, we stuck together."

'I was proud of my uniform too, with the jodhpurs, the coat and the hat. I remember when I went home in it once and there were some boys across the street who shouted, "where is your horse?" I will always remember that and what they must have thought when I came home dressed like that! Everyone else used to wear their hat perched on the back of their head but no, not me. I wore mine straight.'

Mary Harris

Born 28 August 1925; joined the Women's Land Army in 1946

'Well, I actually got thrown off the first farm I went to because I saw the farmer's son pulling the tails of the cows and told him, "Do not do that, it is cruel!" But he didn't listen. There was a birthday cake in a tin on the side, so I threw it over him, and it was then that the farmer suggested I move somewhere, for want of a better phrase, more suited! I just wanted to escape Preston so joined in 1946 and went to Lincolnshire.

'Ah, yes, I have lots of stories, but you would not have enough paper to write them all down. I remember the time there was a water shortage in Lincolnshire and we were only allowed one bath a week. I worked

Mary as a land girl.

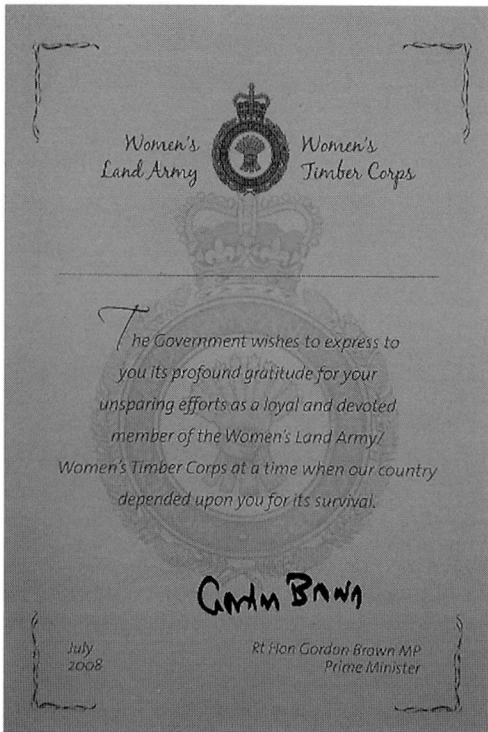

Letter of government acknowledgement to former WLA members.

The Women's Land Army badge.

Mary Harris' paperwork including release certificate and WLA badge.

with the cows, so I was utterly filthy, but all the girls smelt so we smelt together! My bath day? I remember, it was a Wednesday.

'There was also the time the pipes got blocked so I went down to the river for a wash with no costume as I didn't have one, and I went in, you know, as I was. You wouldn't have been able to do that sort of thing back home in Preston, oh no!

'You do these silly things, do you not? But they make for good stories in the end.

'I saw all sorts. I worked with Prisoners of War and I remember there could be ill feeling from people if they were hanging around the hostel, but most of them were just ordinary men, like ours were. Naturally there were some relationships and if there was any hostility, it came from fraternising. Some were even attacked by locals for it.

'I was quite bored in Lincolnshire though, because all I had to do was guard the cows all day. I would just stand there under the trees, watching them, and I needed something more energetic.

'I got moved to Gretford Hall, in Stamford, and that is where I started milking. I really enjoyed it there, and I loved the outdoors. I even met my husband, Abe, there on Valentine's Day in 1946, but after only three

Mary and Abe.

Mary's WLA transfer application letters.

More of Mary Harris' paperwork including WLA club membership and weekly time sheet.

CLUB CHARGES

The annual membership fee is 2s. 6d., payable on your first visit in the year to the Club.

	£	s.	d.
Bed and Breakfast (one night) ...		5	0
Bed and Breakfast (seven nights)	1	10	0
Full Lunch (three courses) ...		1	6
Tea			10
Supper		1	4

Your friends may be invited to meals at an additional charge of 6d. per guest, and are also admitted to the Club's attractive Lounge and Writing Room.

The Club is maintained by the Women's Land Army Benevolent Fund.

YOU ARE INVITED to spend your holiday or week-end in London at the W.L.A. Club.

Sight Seeing !
River Trips !
Theatres !
Dances !

Reservations for accommodation should be made in advance to the Warden.

The Club is open every day to members of the Land Army organisation.   Ex-members of the W.L.A. are also welcome, but can only reserve accommodation from Mondays to Fridays.

Leaflet information on social club activities.

WLA social club leaflet.

weeks, I was posted down to Tiverton in Devon. We spoke about it and agreed that I should just get on with it and go.

'There were girls from everywhere there, just thrust into this new way of life. I especially liked taking care of the horses, feeding them and cleaning them out, and hoeing the fields in summer was nice too, as I liked being out in the sun.

'I remember on one occasion when we had got all dressed up to go out, and all the girls were sat in the back of a big open truck. This particular girl in charge had only just learnt to drive and was trying her best to manoeuvre this gaggle of women along these winding country roads in a big lorry. I was petrified!

'I think my favourite thing was picking sugar beet and slicing the tops off with a large knife. We had to do it in the freezing cold though, and you couldn't use gloves because you had to be able to feel what you were doing.

'Things were very manual at first. I remember going back once and seeing a machine whooshing up and down the field of blackcurrants. But things move on.

'Anyway, I asked to be posted back nearer to Abe, and they denied my request. I went to visit him, and I was late coming back so for this, they sent me to Yaelmpton in Portsmouth, to a punishment house.

'I was so isolated and so far from anywhere. It was a horrible old house with brown water coming out of the taps. I stuck it out for a month but could not do it any longer and I resigned completely. There is no resentment though. There were rules in place, and I broke them.

'It was all exciting at the time and I mixed with so many people. I met miner's daughters from Yorkshire, I met girls from the stage, I met lesbians for the first time in my life and I did not even know they existed! I feel very proud, and it was a positive experience because I learnt to judge people on who they were as human beings rather than anything else.'

Joan Ackrill

Born on 15 March 15, 1930; joined the Women's Land Army in 1947
'I was 17 years old and I can tell you, a brash little Londoner. Along with 19 other brash little women from South-East London, we were sent to Oxfordshire to become Land Girls.

'It was 1947 and up until then most of us had lived in council flats without any window boxes or anything. It was a deprived area and heavily bombed through 1940 and 1941. I don't know what on earth made us think we could farm!

Joan Ackrill with other Land Girls.

'I left home because I was unhappy. What teenager isn't? But there was an element of abuse from my elder brother. It was literally a choice between the Women's Auxiliary Air Force, who took recruits at 17-and-a-half or the WLA who took recruits at 17-and-a-quarter. So, it was the WLA for me. There was not any ambition to work on a farm. It was a means of escape. This was case with about 90 per cent of the girls I met in the various hostels. Only one girl I met actually wanted a career in farming.

'We lived in a hostel that ranged anywhere between 20 and 45 girls, but with such different personalities and all from different backgrounds, we had to compromise quite a lot. I don't recall any serious fisticuffs taking place, but then again, it taught us to live in a give and take environment.

'Despite rationing, we were always fed well there too, and had wardens and housekeepers to help take care of us. There was a cleaner for the rooms, a cook preparing our meals, and although we had to make our beds and keep the rooms tidy, all in all, we did not have a bad life, did we?

'I was transported daily to wherever I was needed and did the hoeing, lifted the sugar beet and helped during the harvest, but I wanted something more fulfilling. I asked if I could retrain to be a milker. I thought it would be more interesting and it certainly was. After a month training in hand milking I went on to work in machine milking and picked up skills about animal husbandry as I went along. I learned through everyday life with the head cowman, just watching him.

'With time, after working on one farm for a long spell, I earned myself a promotion to relief milker. This meant I could relieve the head or under cowman on their day off or at the weekend. I had six farms on my rota all together.

'I loved this and it gave me a real chance to meet new people and adapt to their ways of working. We would get up at 5:30am, have a cup of tea, a slice of toast and jump into the vans to do the 6am milking. We made up our sandwiches for lunch the night before, but we also got a rasher of bacon, an egg and a slice of bread that was cooked by the farmer's wife once the morning round was finished. More often than not the farmer's wife would add some fried potatoes or another egg, and there was always a cooked meal when we returned in the evening.

'I was adopted by farming, I guess. We did the jobs allotted to us to the best of our ability, be it in the field or the milking parlour. We were teased at times, possibly in my case for being a "townie", but I am sure it was not because I was female. That sounds all very political and politics was the last thing on our minds.

'I met my husband, William, in 1949 and he had lived on the same farm for most of his life where his father was head cowman himself, a mechanic and tractor driver. After a date to the pictures our relationship flourished, and we married in 1951, and were given a recently renovated cottage on-farm. Our life began then.

'I had left the Land Army by this point but learned to love the gentler ways of the countryside like discovering the flora and fauna that surrounded us, and gardening. I became a stay-at-home wife. In due course we had two children and spent nine happy years there. We moved to Tackely, in Oxford, and life here, needless to say, has been the best we could ask for.

'I don't think the work we did went unrecognised at all. It was never shouted about, but whenever the subject came up over the years, appreciation was expressed. It was only when we received the WLA medal and certificate that the appreciation was widespread. I personally always felt valued for the work I did.'

'The Milker'

Joyce Oehring

Milking becomes the rhythm of my life
And spaces evenly my days
Unregimented, yet not free,
I accept the even tenor of its ways;
Rise in the mists, with stars for light,
Laved in the coolth of morning air.
The cows file to the byre secure
In faith that food awaits them there.
The white, sweet jet invades the pail
I breathe its richness and the warmth of hay,
Familiar smell of cow my nostril fills
The while on Beauty's flank my head I lay.
The gentleness that war perhaps has taught
To people still aghast at fire and flood and fear
Abides within the deftness and the quiet
The patience learned and manifested here.
Peace in the eyes of calves who early find
Confidence is not misplaced in man
If kinship with all creatures man admits
As only he who will not hurt his fellows can.
Part of a pattern whose taut threads
I slackly grasp, but dimly see,
I am enmeshed in ritual outstripping all known time
That was and is, and while the race persists, will be.

Clare Arnold

Born 30 January 1924; joined the Women's Land Army in 1942
'I remember I saw the Women's Land Army recruitment poster when I was cycling home one day, in 1942 – you know the one with the attractive lady – and felt it just suited me down to the ground. I got back to the house and said to my parents, "By the way, I am, joining the Land Army!" They really were not happy as I was the youngest and was expected to stay at home, but I knew I simply had to do something for the war.

'And I loved it, everything about it. I would finish at the farm, get washed, put my dress on and go dancing. I was only 18; I was young, energetic, curious.

Clare Arnold.

'I worked alone though and used to cycle to the farm as it was only three miles from my home in Stafford. I liked and enjoyed my own company, and actually one of my favourite things was getting up and out early in the morning. I enjoyed the fresh morning smell of the fields. It was just me and my milk float at 6am, delivering while the rest of the world was asleep, and it felt like freedom. I had my pony and this rather large sheepdog from the farm that would follow me all the way until a certain house, where someone would give it a bone and it would trot back home and leave me be.

'We all look for something in life, do we not? And this was an adventure for me. Bear in mind, I had never milked before, so I watched the other men do it all and soon picked it up and became fond of my animals. I loved the warmth of the cows on a cold morning. There were times when you would end up covered in milk, upside down in the gutter after a cow lashed out, but it was all part of the job and we did not know any better.

'Being a Land Girl made me feel better about myself and I suppose I felt more grown up. And although rationed, you still ate better on-farm because you had the eggs and the cream on the top of the milk, of course.

'At 5 feet 4 inches I was only slight when I joined, but I remember I put two and a half stone on within three months, can you believe it! I worked hard all day, out in the fields and milking. I even split my breeches one morning when I jumped back into the milk float!

'It was the making of me, physically and mentally, and if I had the energy I would do it all again. We were so young and probably quite naïve, but we just got on with it and did not think it was anything special. I do not think I have ever met anyone who did not enjoy their time, have you?

'I feel prouder now than ever. Yes, it is only now, looking back, we can see more clearly what it was all about.'

Mary Dryda

Born on 11 February 1926; joined the Women's Land Army in 1944

'I signed up in 1944 and I wanted to join because I already knew about the land. I just loved being outside. I was familiar with everything as my uncle had a farm, you see.

'I stayed at home while a land girl, so I'd use my sisters "sit up and beg bike" to ride there and back each day – five-and-a-half miles each way. I could barely see over the top of it!

'I have always been someone who gets up early though, so I did not mind it – I used to wake up at 4am because you get things done that way. We got 22 shillings for seven days a week, but I just loved being out in the countryside, so it did not matter.

Mary Dryda (left).

'And I love cows. It was always nice and warm in the shippon and there was particular one that I used to call Daisy. They are almost human, just like us, you know? I tell you, that cow would not come in without me and none of the other girls could make her budge. It was a good, healthy life.

'Some of the girls were lazy though, and if they could get out of working, they would, but we had a laugh and were always happy to be with each other. We all set to something in life, but as long as we help each other, we are OK. My dad once said to me, "Always do a good turn, never do a bad one", and that has stuck with me.

'I tell you what I did not like though, the uniform. It was an awful thing! Scratchy! Horrid! I once took my dad's long johns and cut them down to make them fit me, and in the winter, as it was so cold, I would wear them underneath.

'We had some fun times, too, and once a month we would go to Morecombe Winter Gardens straight from work. We took our frocks into the toilets to change. I would have some powder and someone else would have some lipstick and I can remember all the soldiers were huddled over in the corner. I said, "oh come on, we will go and ask them to dance." Well, their faces were a picture! But could they dance? Oh, they were good dancers!

'I think my fondest memory though was Victory in Europe Day and at the time I was on my way home in Flookburgh. Walking up to the square there, everyone who had a piano had put it outside, playing it, and all these soldiers were dancing with the girls, celebrating. People were just going for it on all these pianos! It was a great sight. Yes, that's a good memory. I will always remember that.'

Mollie Rogers

Joined the Women's Land Army in 1944

'When I joined the Women's Land Army, it was the most exciting thing I had ever done up to that point.

'I'd always wanted to work with animals – despite my fear of cows! And I'd always wanted to work outdoors but, little did I know what hard work it would be.

'I was all set to go and board the train at Newcastle to Carlisle, then I got a bus to Ireby, an unknown village to me. But, as I went for the bus, I had been given the wrong times and I had missed the last one. Well, panic set in – what could I do? I had a vision of this irate farmer waiting for me! But I had already been evacuated once to Carlisle and I had some friends who I knew would accommodate me.

'The next morning, I was on my way, feeling nervous about what might be in store for me. I remember that the bus conductor asked me where I was going and said he didn't think it was right for Land Girls to be sent so far off the beaten track. Imagine how worried and wary that made me feel!

'Anyway, I arrived and found I would be working alongside another Land Girl, Dora, from Bolton, Lancashire. She was a very slim girl, but amazingly strong. There was another girl who worked in the house, and we all became good friends.

'That first afternoon I was sent out to bring some cows wearing gumboots and overalls – those boots were essential

Mollie Rogers with another Land Girl.

as the fields were so boggy and I kept losing my boots. There I was, shooing these cows, trying not to seem frightened!

'The next job I was given – and I did this for the rest of the week – was mucking out the large cow byre. Lifting the barrel when it was empty felt like a chore, let alone when it was filled with manure, and as I had to make several trips I was completely exhausted by the end of it. The stalls then had to be swilled out and it felt like my arms had no strength left in them whatsoever.

'There was a cowman, so I didn't have to get involved with the milking or anything, but by the end of the week

Mollie with one of the cows.

I was ready to give up! My hands were in a bad way with broken blisters, and every part of me ached – why didn't I just stick with office work?

'It felt like I'd hardly slept when it was time to get up again. All I heard was cows mooing and chickens clucking at unearthly hours. But I was eventually given a job which I enjoyed. I was to look after some dry cows and heifers on another farm up the fell. I cleaned out the stalls, laid fresh bedding and filled the racks with hay.

'Working single-handedly was hard, especially getting the cows back in to their stalls and fastening them up. I remember one morning I was engaged in all my chores and a man appeared at the door asking if I'd seen any stray sheep. He was from another farm on the fell. He saw what I was doing and said he had everything done by 4:30am! "Early to bed, early to rise" must have been his motto but I think many of the old type farmers were like that.

'Anyway, the weeks went by and there were always other jobs to do out in the fields such as muck spreading. In fact, that was my favourite job to do as I always seemed to experience a great deal of satisfaction when I looked back over a field of scattered manure.

'I recall one Sunday when I had to cycle down to the railway station some seven miles away to bring back some cows which had been in cattle trucks overnight. The journey back seemed endless – cows can be stupid!

'Being at Snittlegarth farm was fun in many respects – we worked hard for long hours, but the good times compensated for the weariness we felt.

'Spring was particularly nice and after work we would walk or cycle into the village to spend our sweet coupons (if we had any left) or visit some nearby villages.

'Dances were held from time to time. The village halls were filled up with everybody having a right good time! And what did it matter if we didn't get home until 1am or 2am? We never minded those long rides home, as there was a crowd of us, and we always had something to laugh and sing about! Plus, there was the Women's Institute and the Young Farmers' Clubs.

'After six months, me, Barbara and Dora decided it was time to move on. We worked long hours and had no time off except Sunday (sometimes). We were entitled to half a day off, but we had to save those up if we wanted to go home for the weekend. Sometimes we'd be working as late as 10pm at night, and there was no extra pay for this. Land Girls were paid £3 per week, and thirty shillings of that went to the farmer for keep.

'I moved on to another dairy farm just outside of Carlisle. It was a very modern farm with a milking parlour installed, the first time I had ever seen one. I had to be up and out in the yard for 6:05am, which I didn't mind, but, oh, the snobbish people I worked for! I got to have my meals with them but after my evening meal, I was expected to go to my room.

'By the end of that week I'd had enough and duly asked for a transfer. Needless to say, the WLA authority weren't too pleased with me, however, they moved me to a dairy farm at Gilsland, on the borders of Cumbria and Northumberland, just 40 miles from my home in Newcastle. And I spent the next 12 months there.

'I took to the people as soon as we met, and to this day I am still in touch with the widow of the man I worked for. I lived with the chap who managed the farm, his wife and wee daughter, and there was also a hired lad living there who'd arrived a few weeks before me. The farm owner lived in a large house next door, but we saw him most mornings when he came to inspect the milk records.

'Work started at 6:30am and finished at 6pm, except in hay time and harvest. There were 23 pedigree Ayrshires to be milked, and I was shown how to use the milking machine and see to the weighing and milk recording of each cow. After milking, all the equipment had to be washed and sterilised. In winter I used to hate rinsing off with cold water as my fingers stuck to the milk churns!

'The cooler and sieves had to be kept scrupulously clean and woe betide if they weren't, as once a month a man from the Milk Marketing Board came to check the records and cleanliness. The byres had to be kept spotlessly clean, walls scrubbed and swilled down – even the cows' tails were washed and brushed, and their udders wiped each morning and evening.

'In between milking I did all sorts of field work depending on the season – muck spreading, lime spreading, gathering turnips, cutting kale. Hay time and harvesting was all go. It was hot, dusty work and I was glad of the breaks at 10am and 3pm when the farmer's wife brought us tea and goodies. It was good to rest with our backs against the haystacks and I have happy memories of riding back to the farm sat on a stack of hay! Then the hard work started again as it was loaded into the barn.

'We worked long hours, and sometimes I'd cycle to another farm after work to help a friend with their haymaking as they worked odd hours. I enjoyed working with the animals, especially the calves. Bull calves weren't kept very long. They were taken for slaughter pretty quickly which made me sad. Then again, if a cow got too sick to recover or too old, I was sad. I remember one, old Hazel, she had bad feet and could hardly walk, and the wagon came for her one morning. And I remember killing pigs very well. I can remember the awful squealing as it was led away, and for a long time I couldn't face bacon or black pudding that I'd helped the farmer's wife to make!

'Agricultural shows were always an occasion. Some of our stock was entered, of course – Blossom the Clydesdale, some sheep, calves and a heifer called Barbara who I trained to walk for weeks before. She got to be rather a pet and would run across the field when I called her name, but she knew I always had nuts to feed her! Barbara seemed to know something

Mollie was a Land Girl for
2 years.

was afoot and I imagined her careering across the field uncontrollably, however, we managed to give her a shampoo and dry her down.

'Show day was a great day with farming families arriving from the surrounding areas and those from "out by" – what we called the farms on the fell. At long last judging commenced! And we were delighted when Barbara and Blossom won in their respective classes! It was a long day and we were too tired to attend the show dance, but some of those farmers could dance as light as feathers in their boots!

'In the spring of 1946 the German PoWs arrived, 17 of them, all high-ranking officers who were transported every day by bus to do fieldwork from Featherstone Camp near Haltwhistle. I saw very little of them apart from when their cook came to the dairy for water. He told me a lot about his family, where he'd been captured, and how he longed to return to his country. I remember they were very fond of flowers, and one day they asked the owner of the farm if they could pick some for someone's birthday back at the camp. He said yes and they were able to pick from over 40 different types of daffodil.

'I remember so clearly the day victory over Japan was announced. I had been sent into Brampton, 17 miles away, to collect something, only to find on my return that the buses had stopped running due to celebrations. I had to borrow a bike and cycle back, all uphill! Once at the top though, it was all plain sailing from there and I had the most wonderful view of all the bonfires that had been lit for VJ day. Back at the farm, it was a rush to get dressed and ready for the dance at the village hall that had been organised quickly to celebrate. I don't know where I got the energy from, but I did, and I still got up at 6:30am the next morning!

'After a hard day's work, most evenings were spent knitting or listening to the wireless or talking. However, on Saturdays there was a dance in the village hall – we did the usual dances but learnt some modern ones such as "Three drops of brandy" and "Gay Gordons"! They were all very energetic but very fun!

'Sometimes the farmer and his wife would entertain their friends with supper, and we'd be invited, and everyone always had plenty to talk about as there was no television. One special evening that I do recall was the "Miss Agriculture" competition. I was fortunate to be one of the six finalists but that was as far as I got.

'The only real unpleasant experience I recall was catching ringworm. Me and another girl had treated some infected cattle, caught it and had to go for ultra-violet-ray treatment which worked the first time. But after a month it came back! It eventually healed and disappeared, but we used to go to dances wearing long-sleeved dresses or blouses to cover the unsightly rings!

'The time came, though, when I decided to leave and return to my old job in a solicitor's office. It was June 1946, and so I left the farm where I'd spent so many happy months. I'd met so many friends and great people and had the experience of working on the land which gave me great satisfaction. I had enjoyed doing my little bit towards the war effort and my memories of my days in the Women's Land Army will stay with me forever.'

Land Girls leaving the forestry training camp at 8am in 1943 in Suffolk. Aerial view of the dormitories, bath hut, canteen and recreation room.

Lumberjills sitting an examination as part of their training in 1943. (*Wikimedia*)

Dorothy Lacey had been bombed in Bristol and in Bath before joining the WLA in Northampton at the Institute of Agriculture. Here she is preparing chicken feed. (*Wikimedia*)

Land girls returning to their barracks at 5pm after working in the forest in Suffolk 1943. (*Wikimedia*)

Two WLA members harnessing a horse at the training centre in Cannington 1940. (*Wikimedia*)

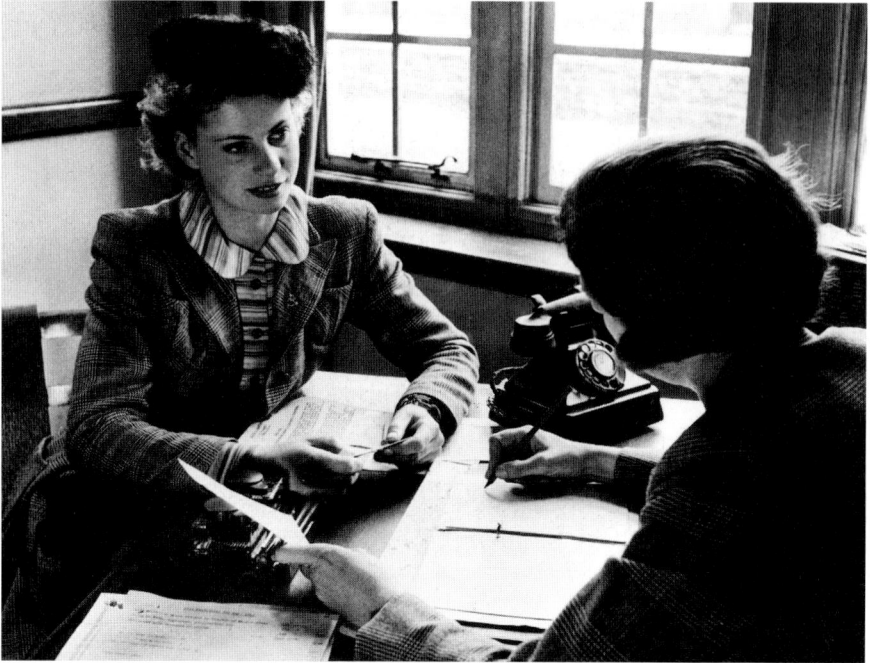

Iris Joyce ,19, with a recruiting officer enrolling into the WLA in 1942. (*Wikimedia*)

Two WLA members clearing out the pig sty in 1940. (*Wikimedia*)

Feeding geese was part of the training at the WLA centre in 1940. (*Wikimedia*)

Here, kitchen staff member, Barbara Smaile, is bringing in the bread at the WLA rest break house in Torquay. (*Wikimedia*)

Four women sharing a bedroom at the WLA rest break house in Torquay in 1944. (*Wikimedia*)

Here is some of the equipment used by the WLA rat catching members. (*Wikimedia*)

Here, the Duchess of Gloucester chats with women of the Australian Land Army. (*Wikimedia*)

'War, which has brought to others fear'

Hebe Jerrold, Women's Timber Corps

War, which has brought to others fear,
Pain, sorrow, slavery, death,
To me has brought what I held dear,
And longed for but could not possess.
Has given me wide stretch of sky,
The sailing clouds, the wind's sharp breath,
A roof of leaves, the wild flower's eye,
Bird song, all woodland loveliness,
Health, vigour, deep content, and faith
That at its source our stream runs clear.
What have I done? I never meant
To be a war-time profiteer!

Sylvia Harper

Born on 17 December 1926; joined the Women's Land Army in 1944

'I had wanted to join the Land Army since I was 13 years old, after being evacuated to East Anglia where my foster mother was a Land Girl on the farm there. I used to come home from school and meet her – she drove a tractor, usually lifting sugar beet.

'When I went home to Belvedere, which had been bombed badly, I had to do war work, so my cousin Robo and I became domestic staff at the local cottage hospital.

'When I was 16 I applied to the WLA and said I was 17! But they said I was too young and to apply in a years' time – which I did.

Sylvia Harper in her Land Girl's uniform.

Sylvia (right) with her cousin in Trafalgar Square.

'The day I went to the church hall to be measured up for my uniform was a great day, and I was told to report to Swadelands, in Lenham, Kent, that evening – one of a number of large houses that had been converted into a Land Army hostel and stripped of all its finery!

'I was lucky being sent to a hostel. There were about 40 girls there. My uniform was delivered in two kitbags, and I served the matron at the hospital her last lunch, put my uniform on and went to wait for the train. Robo was already in Lenham and had left six months before me.

'The corduroy breeches, emerald-green jerseys, cream shirts, brown shoes and long, woollen socks made me feel very glamourous, but I really fancied myself in the famous bush hat! However, it was hardly recognisable as a hat when I pulled it out from the kitbag, crushed. But I soon pushed the crown in, steamed a sharp crease, stitched the cords on the band and tied it under my chin. On Dartford station I felt like a real rookie, joined by other girls going to Lenham.

'The house was ruled sternly by Miss Paris, the matron, and we had to abide by the rules. All clothes and boots had to be left in special rooms at the back, and when we wore our walking out clothes we could use the front door. Our hostel had a sitting room and on cold nights a fire was lit to welcome us in from the cold, but it only had two chairs! I remember two sisters who worked on a private farm always occupied these because they got home earlier than us. They sat tight in these chairs all evening and we all had to sit on the floor! We called them the mutton sisters!

'Our day started at six in the morning, with a member of the hostel staff banging a wooden spoon on a frying pan at the front door of the galleried staircase.

'Apart from a few girls, we all worked for the Kent War Agricultural Committee – we were called "the gang". Harry Boy, our lorry driver, took us to the farms that needed us.

'We had a good social life too – an occasional ENSA party came to entertain us or we organised our own dances in Lenham at the institute, which were always a success.

'A lot of land girls lived on the farms with the farmer's family and were not always welcome to sit with them in the evenings, so they had to stay in their cold bedrooms. They had no social life and if they lived in Wales or Yorkshire, they were usually miles away from a town and couldn't go home at weekends. They were really hard done by.

Sylvia with "the gang".

'Some girls were given a farm cottage to live in and they catered for themselves – this would have been disastrous for us as we were given a pound of jam each month for sandwiches, but usually ate it in a day or so! We went without for the rest of the month with just margarine and bread.

'Once a month there was a meeting in the matron's office to air any grievances. We were always given two slices of bread spread thinly with butter in our lunch tins. When it was my turn to be spokesman my friend, Ethel, said I was to suggest that we only had one slice of bread spread thickly with butter and when I finally plucked up the courage to ask, I was told not to be so ridiculous!

'I was engaged to an airman who was demobbed and living in Bearsted, a small village in Kent, so was transferred to Weavering House. I was not happy there. I didn't like the girls who were all new recruits and bossy, but being close to Maidstone was nice and Bearsted was only a mile away. The matron, Miss Chinchen, was a very good cook and when I left in July 1948 she gave me a cookbook called 'Cooking for Brides, Bachelors and Beginners.' I still have that now.

Sylvia working and enjoying life as a Land Girl.

Slyvia Harper did various jobs on farms.

Slyvia worked as part of a group.

'Swadelands is no longer there, and there are some very nice detached houses in its place. I passed by these recently and noticed the pine trees and bushes were left, still close to the road. I smiled to myself as I remembered the matron banging her wooden spoon on the frying pan at ten at night, calling out into the darkness, "Come in land girls! Go home soldiers!" What a story those trees and bushes could tell!

'I left the Land Army in July 1948 when I got married, but will never forget those days. Nor have I forgotten "the gang". We still keep in touch after all this time, but death has thinned our ranks.'

Sylvia's wedding day.

Betty Smith

Born on 29 December 1925; joined the Women's Land Army in 1941

'It always makes me laugh when people talk about farm school or training because I did not get any. We were just told to report to such and such a place – we did not even have a uniform.

'My sister joined The Auxiliary Territorial Service, but I was only 16 and they would not take you so young. I heard you could be a Land Girl at 17, so I signed up. And, I guess I lied about my age!

'I could not wait to get away, as there really was not much more than cotton mills surrounding me in the Lake District.

'I got transferred to Hertfordshire and I think all the work I did on the farm stood me in good stead you know, because I can still get down and touch my toes and all that now. Everything was done by hand. People ask me if I have got aches and pains but I'm fine. I am very independent.

Betty Smith in a truck with her friends.

'In the Land Army you just had to get on with it. You were simply expected to do or know things, even if you had never done it before. I remember on one occasion when they asked me to go and work on a farm temporarily to cover the milking duties and the woman there asked me to kill a chicken. I said "no, I am not doing that". I could not. But they just assumed you had done these things. I enjoyed working on the threshing machine, though, because you did not get quite as dirty.

'I don't think anybody minded us doing these jobs, and if there was any bad feeling towards us I was immune to it. I did not, and still do not, bother about what other people are saying.

'You may have found that the farmer might have tried to embarrass you sometimes, asking you to hold the sheep down while they were castrated, even though they were too strong for us to do so, but I liked the company and made lots of friends. There was a nice atmosphere in the hostel plus, you got to have a bath every night!'

Invoice and receipt from 1943.

Land Girl Edith Mole.

Edith Mole's sister Joan was also a Land Girl.

Edith (right) with another Land Girl.

Edith Mole with her husband John Boyce.

Joan Mole's release certificate.

Land Girls enjoying a cup of tea on a farm in Sussex after a day of rat catching. (*Wikimedia*)

New Land Girl recruits in Nottinghamshire. (*Wikimedia*)

Land Girls pulling turnips in a field in Kendal, Lake District. (*Wikimedia*)

Land Girls collecting the crop in Llandrillo. (*Wikimedia*)

Land Army recruitment poster. (*Wikimedia*)

Land Girl on a training farm in Cannington. (*Wikimedia*)

Mary Snowden

Born on 25 December 1924; joined the Women's Land Army in 1941

<u>*This excerpt was originally found on The Women's Land Army*</u>

'At the age of 17 I was driving around the villages of Kent in my own tractor, enjoying the freedom and independence of being in the Women's Land Army. It was 1942, and I enlisted to escape Canterbury after the terrible bombing in which many people were killed, including two of the nurses from the hospital where I had previously worked. They had gone out to a tea-room in the city and never returned for their shift that evening.

'I enlisted as a Land Girl with a friend when I was 16 in 1941. I remember that I didn't even have to get my parent's permission! We were sent to Plumpton near Lewes for our six-week assessment and training, during which we were tested out on various aspects of farming during the day, and sat through films and lectures during the evening. I remember helping to hold down the cows for the bull's visit while attempting dairy farming and deciding this was not for me, but I enjoyed learning to drive a tractor and understanding some of the mechanics, such as how to change a gasket.

'It seemed second nature to sit up in the driving seat, steering in a straight line or learning to pull a trailer. There were road bands to fix around the rubber wheels so that the tractor could be driven along tarmacked roads, and we had to understand the difference in types of fuel. When I was working in

Land Girl Mary Snowden.

the fields my tractor ran on TVO (tractor vapourising oil), but petrol was used to start the engine and warm it up.

'My main job was to help with flax pulling. Flax was essential to the war effort as it was used in parachute harnesses and the seed was made into linseed oil, so I drove around to farms all over mid-Kent from Pluckley to Cudham – to wherever I was needed. The flax was taken to the English Flax Company factory in Pluckley. There it was pressed through rollers and separated into strands ready to be woven into material and the seeds made into oil. I was part of a busy process which was hard work but never seemed dull.

'I was chosen to be one of two Land Girls who were picked to work in the factory full-time after the harvest was over. We had to collect the stooks of flax which lorries had brought to the factory to be stored in great Dutch barns, and then drive our load exactly under the elevator. It was a tricky procedure backing in a four-wheel trailer to get it in just the right place. In the factory I used a rubber-tyred tractor which ran on petrol, as it had to stop and start quite often. Once the flax had been processed by the machines in the factory, we then had to transport it to Pluckley Station.

Mary working on a tractor.

'The best part for me was harvest time in the summer. I loved the freedom of travelling through the country lanes to my next job as the Kent countryside was so beautiful and I loved being in the open air. I boarded in the village of Egerton, but during the harvest stayed on the farms where I was working. Tasks and billets were assigned by the Crops Officer, who would meet me regularly and tell me where I would be stationed next. I arrived at a farm, took the road bands off my tractor and then drove up and down the fields in straight lines, with a machine behind my tractor which pulled the flax out of the ground and tied it in sheaves. I had to take care at the corners to reverse and cover the whole field. It was mainly older men and teenagers not yet enlisted who actually gathered the flax sheaves into stooks, so that it could be collected by lorries which would take it to the factory. There was some banter and a little flirting! One young boy became so besotted with me that he sent a box of apples to my home every year for some time after I left his farm.

'From week to week I never knew exactly where I would end up, and that was part of the fun of the job. I remember my Crops Officer asking me if I had any nice frocks as I would be staying with a farmer called Mr Freeman, of Freeman, Hardy and Willis, the shoe company, and the family expected me to dress for dinner. Wherever I was billeted, the farmer usually treated me as one of the family, so we all ate together at the end of the day, with better food than I would have had in the hospital digs. Although the farmers had to give up their produce for the war effort, no one could count the number of eggs a chicken laid, nor the apples on a tree. There was always fresh butter and milk, and I can still remember homemade lemonade being brought out to the fields when I was thirsty on a hot, dusty day. Sometimes the farmers would shoot the rabbits that were exposed in the fields when the flax was pulled. Although I didn't enjoy skinning and paunching them, they made tasty meals!

'Even better than the food, on rare occasions there was a hot bath, and a chance to dress up for a dance in one of the parish halls. At that time of the war there were large numbers of enlisted men billeted in that part of Kent, so it was a great time to be young and female! I don't think I would have had the same freedom and independence living at home, but the demands of the work helped me learn to look after myself.

'Looking back, I can't remember any grey rainy days. The sun always seemed to be shining, which seems ironic now as we were going through some of the darkest days of the war.'

Joan Harburn Hall

The following account is taken from 'My Land Army Life', a book written by the late Joan Harburn Hall.

Born on 28 April 1922; joined the Women's Land Army in 1942
'I was born in Huddersfield but spent much of my childhood visiting Penrith. As war clouds gathered and broke in 1939, friends and relatives left to become members of the armed forces. At 17 I began to wonder, what did life have in store for me?

'The factory floor wasn't for me. I wanted the freedom and open-air life of a Land Girl so I returned the application forms with a special request to be posted to the Newton Rigg Farm School to be trained, having spent time there when I was younger with my nanny, Mrs Jackson, whom I adored.

'Never in my wildest dreams did I think it would happen, but it did, and in 1942 I was a fully-fledged member. And so, then started a series of adventures that I still find very hard to believe!

'The day of departure came, and I made my way to the station, arriving in Penrith. I joined all the other recruits in a large hall where all of us were summing each other up. It was the first time I had heard so many different accents – Geordie, Scouse, Brummie – but they would all become familiar soon, though.

'I shared a dorm with five other girls, two of whom, Lottie and Joyce, became my friends. We made quite the trio! The three musketeers getting into many a scrape!

'Girls took it in turns to make tea and there was a rota for washing up. I used to get cigarettes sent from home, and as I didn't smoke I could exchange them and get out of washing up. What some people would do for a cigarette always surprised me!

'Anyway, once training had finished, I was posted to Gill House, just outside Aspatria near the Cumberland coast. It had been a large mansion with a farm attached, sat at the end of a long, dark drive covered with overhanging trees. At night, all the girls waited at the gate for a companion to walk with as venturing down alone was unheard of.

'I shared a room with four girls and in there was what looked like a built-in wardrobe that turned out to be a rather long passage, used in days gone by for a cloakroom. There were a number of pictures in it, including that of a naked man. We used to joke that we had a man in our bedroom!

'Every day trucks would come and take us to where we were needed, and we would sing as loud as we could, heralding our coming you could say.

'Our jobs were varied. At that time the fields were full of golden, waving corn and feathery barley which we had to stack into stooks in straight rows after the binder had been around the field. Your hands got full of thistles, and it was a full-time job to get them out with a sharp needle. We did all get a nice tan though, and we were the envy of all our friends back in the towns.

'Harvesting was something I really enjoyed. Each sheaf of corn had to be laid the correct way and the key was to be quick. The more experienced farm hands then thatched the top to keep out the weather and preserve it.

'Yes, most of the farmers and farm hands endured our efforts with patience and although we endured a lot of teasing and leg pulling, we all got along well on the whole. All the girls came from every walk of life. Helen, my good friend, had been brought up in a convent and learnt how to be a lady. She knew how to dance and had all the social graces, but like everyone else, had to change her way of life.

'We used to go to the dances held at the local village hall. Most of us had to go in uniform and dancing in brogues became an acquired art! I remember a time when me and Helen met two boys who we knew weren't local because of their accents. They were working on a neighbouring farm and were conscientious objectors. But we enjoyed their company and we used to make it back to the hostel on the back of their motorbikes!

'I was reposted numerous times, first to a gardening position at Braithwaite just outside Keswick, then to a stately home at Plumpton, near Penrith. The dances at Plumpton were occasions that nobody liked to miss, and one night I was given permission to stay until the end. But like Cinderella, the clock struck midnight and I was at least ten minutes late home and locked out. So, I cycled six miles back to Mrs Jackson's in Penrith and threw stones at her window.

'Well, the next morning I went to see the WLA secretary and told her I wasn't going back to Plumpton. After Christmas they posted me to a Forestry Commission Hostel in Grasmere, but I just looked at the barren piece of ground that I was expected to cultivate, and at the horrible wintery conditions and decided there and then that horticulture wasn't for me.

'After that, head office decided I wasn't to be trusted with a "responsible job" and sent me as far up the fellside as they could. Another Land Girl, Connie, was my keeper and tasked with keeping me on the straight and narrow, but it should have been the other way around really – Connie had committed "an indiscretion" three years earlier by having a child.

'We worked for the Hope family who did all the threshing for the district. Little did anyone know that though they thought they were punishing me by sending there I was to spend the happiest days of my Land Army life there. I remember I used to get teased mercilessly about my Yorkshire accent, and it took me a long time to get used to the Cumbrian dialect.

'Sometimes we spent a week in the same village depending on how many farms needed their corn and barley threshed, always starting our morning with rashers of thick, fatty bacon. Many farms would always have great sides of bacon or hams hung in the kitchen, and at the bottom of the garden was pig ready to be killed, but thankfully not while I watched.

'We always managed to cycle back to Penrith at the weekends for the Saturday night dances at Drill Hall, riding on the baskets of our bikes as some gallant youth peddled away! Our life was in their hands really, but it was easier than walking.

'I did all sorts from then on. The next farm we were to help on I got the chance to learn how to drive. It was an old car converted into a small lorry and used to carry manure down to the fields. I had to stand on the back with a fork and throw manure into the ploughed furrows. I couldn't work fast enough though and had to swap with the farm hand and drive the car. You can imagine what happened. I didn't steer the car straight and the jerking movements threw the farm hand right into the manure. Sure enough, we swapped right back!

'I also learnt to milk my first cow here. Most of the herd were black Aberdeen Angus with beautiful faces and gentle manners. I used to think that all black cows were bulls which I quickly learnt wasn't the case!

'One day I mentioned to the local vicar that I'd never been christened and with no more ado, he said that had to remedied right away. So, I was christened on 8 July 1943, aged 19, with the vicar as my godfather and Mrs Jackson as my godmother!

'I was eventually posted to Scaleby House, Carlisle, which wasn't a happy place. But I was in the throes of romance with my future husband, Edmund. He was a marvellous dancer and we finally got engaged in August 1943. We set our wedding date to correspond with Edmund's leave, and were married on 10 November 1943. In March, morning sickness took hold and I left the Land Army to go back to Huddersfield to have my daughter, Angela.

'Memories of my time come flooding back, bringing waves of nostalgia with them, and a yearning to be back there once again, to taste the bit of freedom I had.'

'Challenge'

by Enid Barraud, Cambridgeshire

Let's take the joy our misery has earned,
Snatching our kisses while life's back is turned.
We'll be such splendid lovers, you and I,
Tossing gay laughter to the summer sky,
We'll halve Life's apple with a knife and share it,
Savouring it on our lips,
And hand Life back, upon a silver salver,
The pips!

Jeanne Dorothy Sellings

Born on 21 July 1923; joined the Land Army in 1942

'I was born and raised in Tunbridge Wells, and when I joined the Women's Land Army at 19 years of age, I was stationed near home and could ride my bike back to visit my parents. They were supportive of my decision to join, and my father was a volunteer in air raid shelters.

'I can remember the air raids. I would have to lie in a ditch until it was over. My mother refused to go to a shelter, telling us that if it was her time to die, she would die in her own bed.

'But I remember my Land Army days with complete fondness. I hadn't really done any farming in the past, but my father was the gardener at a big hotel in Tunbridge Wells called The Spa. It's still there.

Jeanne in her Land Girl uniform.

Jeanne with her Land Girl friends.

'I worked hard, but at times worked in a big house for a wealthy family where I would have to lay out the gentleman's clothes for him!

'I do remember once when we were shovelling hay, there were so many rats in the barn where I was working. A rat somehow got into my overalls and I had to shake it out through my pant leg! The girls laughed and laughed at me!

'I made a lifelong friend in the WLA. Her name was Audrey and we always kept in touch through letters. I felt empowered and independent during my time there and was very proud of my service, but to me it was just something that I thought was the right thing to do.

'I met my husband, Joseph, while in the WLA, too. He was in the United States Navy and was driving a truck with another sailor and picked up a bunch of Land Girls for a dance we were all attending. Apparently, as soon as he saw me he told his friend, "I want to get to know the little dark-haired girl!" At the same time, I was telling my friend that I wanted to meet the driver. It was love at first sight.

'We were married on 25 August 1945 in Tunbridge Wells, and Joseph left England after the war and finished his time in the navy in November 1945. I, a new war bride, came to the United States on the SS *Argentina*. It left Southampton and arrived at New York Harbour on 4 February

Jeanne and her husband Joseph.

Jeanne and Joseph shortly after arriving in New Jersey.

1946. It was the first ship of English war brides to the US. There were 456 wives and 170 babies on board. It was a nine-day voyage and there were terrible storms. It felt as though the ship was a cork in the water getting tossed around. I was pregnant with my first child, Jane, who was born in June 1946. I was seasick the entire time, along with everyone else on board!

'I was also the first war bride to New Jersey and the newspaper did a story on me. We lived with Joseph's family when I first arrived, but it was very different for me because I was an only child! He had a brother and seven sisters, and they all lived together, ranging in ages from seven to 21. It was quite a culture shock for me to suddenly have all these siblings.

'One year for our wedding anniversary Joseph gave me a beautiful gold charm bracelet. The charm was a heart shape that said "Love at first sight" to remind us of those wartime days and how we met.

'We went on to have five children – four girls and a boy – and I worked as a waitress for many years in an upscale restaurant.

'Unfortunately, I never returned to England and kept in touch [with those at home] by weekly letters. I would have loved to go back for a visit, but the finances just didn't allow it. My parents did come to the United States for a long visit in 1972, but sadly it was the only time I got to see them in all those years'.

Doreen Dallaire

Born on 4 October 1920; joined the Women's Land Army in 1939

'I grew up in Rye, a village about 55 miles southeast of London, in Sussex. I was one of six children, and shortly before Britain entered into the war, my father passed away. In order to pay off the doctor's bill, my mother had to pick hops. I helped and picked an umbrella-full every day until the bill was paid.

'As the war progressed, I remember the many times we were woken from our sleep by the air raids. I used to get scared as the bombs dropped and would run into the cupboard. We never went into the shelters because my mother didn't want to mix with the village folk!

'There was a feeling of panic among the women in the village when news came that Hitler had landed in France. However, my attitude was

Doreen with another Land Girl.

one of, well there's nothing we can do if a bomb hits us, so I decided to go about my routine.

'Eventually, I wanted to do my bit for the war effort and joined the Women's Land Army in 1939. Of course, my mother was not pleased with the idea and thought I wasn't physically capable to work the land.

'Being in the Women's Land Army was the biggest turning point in my life. In joining I was given the experience of working on farms. One time I worked on a chicken farm, I cleaned out rabbit cages on another and would dig the ground up for planting – really hard ground.

'Robertsbridge in East Sussex was my last posting. We named it 'Doodle-bug Alley' because the flying bombs which Hitler sent over to aim at London made a weird rumbling sound as they fell.

'I developed a good friendship here, though, with Beth. We shared a room and became very close during that posting. Every day we both cycled to work, 8am to 5pm with a half hour for lunch and a small break in the afternoon.

'My job was to stand by the threshing machine and feed the wheat using a long stick to allow for smooth feeding. At the end of most days we came home to a good meal and spent the rest of my evenings quietly because I felt exhausted from the work.

'When I left the Land Army, I missed our group of women, but me and Beth still kept in touch.

'The war brought tragedy to my family though, when we were told that my brother Fred's ship had been bombed and he was presumed dead. This devastated my mother and she was never the same after that. I remember him coming home on leave and telling me about his world travels.

'The war did bring one bright spot to an otherwise routine way of life – a very handsome French-Canadian man caught my heart!

'I met John in the village shop in 1940 near Robertsbridge, as he was stationed nearby. I was never too tired to meet my John after my day of threshing was over.

'When we got married I left the Women's Land Army and returned home to stay with my mother while John was posted all over, including Belgium, France, and Germany.

'Unfortunately, when our first born arrived, John was away but my sister, Mollie, helped me.

Doreen with her husband John.

Doreen and John with their first child.

'At the height of the war, Rye was subjected to many air raids and the local theatre where my other sister, Lil, worked was completely destroyed, killing one man. I remember, if that bomb had dropped in the afternoon, I would have lost Lil too. Life carried on, and I just waited for the war to end while looking after the baby.

'After the war, John went back to Canada to settle things and told me that he'd send for us. I used to love to play the gramophone and would listen to "Springtime in the Rockies" without imagining I would one day be going to this beautiful country! I went to Canada in 1946 by ship, the famous *Queen Mary* and took the train from Halifax to Montreal. I remember thinking that the bread tasted like cake after being used to rations! Finally arriving in Montreal, I wondered about my future as what greeted me were stairs thick with dust and my father-in-law trying to clean the four-room apartment!'

Sarah Margaret Stanyer

Born on 16 September 1927; joined the Women's Land Army in 1946
'My knowledge of farming was not great by any means. My father, who was a lead miner, kept a few cattle and chickens on our smallholding, and one pig which would be fattened, butchered and preserved in a salt bath before the sides of meat would be hung from hooks along the beams in the scullery and provide ham and bacon for the family over the winter.

'I was 18 at the time, living at home in Penyfford, near Holywell, Wales, with my parents and aunt. My sister, who was 14 years older than me, left to get married while I was still very young.

'I desperately wanted to join The Women's Land Army, but I worked at Courtaulds factory in Flint and it was considered essential war work in parachute production. I helped to move heavy bales of silk around the

Margaret (as she was known) driving the Ferguson tractor at Ty Gwyn, 1948.

factory to and from the washing area; the bales were piled high on pallets and then lifted and moved with a forklift truck. This would normally have been considered "a man's work", but the men were all away fighting and therefore the work was carried out by women and a few men deemed too old to go to war. In 1945/46, when the men started to return to their homes and their jobs, I was finally released from my factory duties and allowed to pursue a career of my choosing.

'I had ideas of joining the Women's Land Army somewhere in Kent or the South Coast, as far away as possible from home which was out in the countryside, and far from the nearest town or any sort of social life. There was no motorised transport at home, so to meet up with my cousins and friends, I had to cycle several miles.

'But my other reason for wanting to join The Women's Land Army was to learn to drive, as there would be little or no chance that I would learn if I had stayed at home. I eventually persuaded my father to allow me to join up, and he agreed on one condition – that I would be posted no more than 15 miles away from home. That would then enable me to come home every couple of weeks. I was duly signed up at Plas Hafod, Gwernymynydd, near Mold, and posted to a farm in Tremeirchion, a small village on the outskirts of St Asaph in North Wales. My lack of farming experience did not worry me in the slightest – I was about to follow a dream which had been out of my reach for so long and I was now ready for anything that was thrown my way.

'And so, my life at Ty Gwyn Farm began. I had a very large bedroom in the farmhouse, all to myself, and was treated like a member of the family. I did all sorts of work on the farm, from mucking out the animals to tractor driving and helping out with the harvest. I also helped school new Women's Land Army recruits who were sent to Ty Gwyn to learn the ropes before they were moved on to other farms. These girls were billeted at a hostel in nearby St Asaph. My social life improved too – I had a couple of boyfriends who worked on neighbouring farms.

'The family I worked for consisted of Samuel Stanyer, his wife, Emily, and their son, Lawrence, his wife and two children. Lawrence had three brothers who all farmed in the local area – Norman, Jim and Joe – and when it came to harvest time the farmers and workers from all four farms came together to work as a big team. One time, I went to one of the other

Stooking bales, 1948 – Ann Stanyer (Pat's sister), Peggy Stanyer and Margaret.

Operating the threshing machine, 1948.

family farms with the rest of the workers to help out at threshing time and I met Jim's son, Patrick.

'I liked him a lot, but he had a wicked sense of humour. The worst trick he played on me was to put a cap on my head filled with several field mice he had collected throughout the day. There was lots of loud screaming and Patrick's mother was horrified at what he had done. To try and make me feel better I was invited to stay behind when the rest of the workers went back to their various homes, and allowed a hot soak in the bath – a rare luxury as not many farmhouses had bathrooms in those days. I got to stay and have tea with the family too. After this Patrick was instructed to take me back home to Ty Gwyn. Romance blossomed after that, and we eventually got married in December 1949.

'It was an interesting time for courtship as rationing was still very much ruling people's lives and livelihoods. Fuel was very restricted, and it was not possible to use it for any journey unless it was to transport livestock, for example. On the odd weekend when Pat took me to see my parents,

Pat and Margaret threshing at Ty Ucha, 1948.

Margaret and one of the sheepdogs at Ty Ucha, 1950.

there was usually a calf on the back seat of the Austin car, so if we did get stopped, we could just say we were transporting livestock!

'I loved every minute of my Land Army days and it changed my life. We started our married life living in a council house about a mile away from Ty Ucha Farm where Pat's parents and younger sister lived. Pat would go off to work early each day and not come home until dark, and during the first year of our marriage I continued with Land Army work until early in 1951 when I suffered a miscarriage. A year later, in May 1952, our daughter Susan was born, followed by Jane in November 1955, and finally our son Paul in January 1959.

'In 1965 we moved into Ty Ucha Farm when Pat's parents retired. I worked hard as a farmer's wife, but also helped supplement the family income by working a few evenings a week as a nurse warden at the local hospital in St Asaph. I enjoyed looking after the young nurse cadets who were living apart from their families for the first time, just as I had done 20 years previously, and I would always make sure they were all safely in their beds and accounted for before returning home to my own family.'

'The Threshing Morn'

Audrey Hewlett, East Sussex

The farm to-day is full of stirring life.
The wheat, that fell beneath the binder's knife
And stood in rows of sheaves on ground close shorn
Two weeks or more, now greets the threshing morn.
The threshers do not stay to break their fast,
But set to work, until a plain repast
Is brought in baskets to the scene of toil.
They care not if the food be grimed with oil
Or with the dust that covers hands and face,
But all sit down within a grassy space;
And, rising from the treetops while they eat,
The sun gives promise of the coming heat.
The great machine is started once again,
And soon a sack grows heavy with the grain,
The empty chaff comes pouring to the ground,
And all the air is filled with dust and sound.
While scorching rays beat down on back and head,
From hour to hour the monster must be fed;
The toilers dare not pause, but work apace,
As sweat makes patterns on each dusty face,
And throats are dry with thirst and eyes are sore,
Yet still the hungry giant craves for more.
The sun burns pitiless in cloudless sky,
And, while the stack of straw is mounting high,
The corn-rick slowly sheds its close-packed sheaves;
And eyes stray longingly towards the leaves;
Which spread a cooling shade upon the grass
That looks more tempting as the minutes pass.

Then boys bring jugs of lemonade and tea
And hand them up above the golden sea
Of straw and corn; and as the workers drink,
The knife and pitchfork cast aside, they drink,
The nectar of the gods was no more rare
Than these plain, earthly liquids that they share,
Till everything is drained except the dregs.
The, once more rising on their weary legs,
The slaves of the machine must play their parts,
Exert their failing strength and steel their hearts,
For from the stack the sheaves will soon be gone;
And then – the peace that follows work well done!
The dragon's hunger-pangs at last subside,
And now the farmer, with a glow of pride,
Surveys the sacks that bulge with goodly corn
And covers them against the dewy morn.
The labourers, with hot and aching feet
Trudge slowly to the farm, to wash and eat,
And everyone will early seek his bed,
Worn out by working for the nation's bread;
Soon every window is bereft of light;
The farm sleeps soundly through a quiet night.

Marjorie Walker

Born in 1922; joined the Women's Land Army in 1940

'It was the 18-year-olds that the government said had to join one of the forces which was either the munitions or land army, and of course, me being a country girl and always living in the countryside, I applied for the WLA.

'Dad and mum lived at Stocks Reservoir in Slaidburn, Lancashire, as my dad was reservoir keeper, and I helped with that.

'When I applied for the WLA, I asked if I could stay on with the local farmer who grew some potatoes and oats.

'The land girls who had worked before me were what I called 'townies' who worked for three weeks or so, and they left or were always swapping.

'I was a land girl for about three or four years. I had my own transport and went to collect the tractors – it was all pretty local. I worked on nearly every farm in the valley, from Whitewell to Tosside.

'I met a lot of people, and I was always well treated. I remember on one farm, the farmer would always come out with a great big mug of tea, and on another one, they would bring a big wooden tray out with a doily on, china cups and scones. It wasn't just something in a bag! If the farmer's wife saw me getting back on the tractor she'd shout, "don't start up again!" because it was feeding time and obviously food was scarce.

'In those days, the farmers were thankful even just to have a chatter, because getting about wasn't easy, you know. I didn't mind the uniform either, I had to wear something similar working with dad at the reservoir – in those days we'd have to go out and catch a rabbit and come home with one over each shoulder.

'The life fitted me, even the good, bad and indifferent weather. It never bothered me – my hair was natural at the time and as for make-up, well, I never have used it! There was no set day off, you did things when things needed doing – you know, like cutting the grass for hay or planting potatoes.

'We liked to get together in the village hall in Slaidburn, you know. The teenagers and I got involved in some of the musical productions. I used to love getting together – boys and girls alike – and getting our bikes out. Oh, I've cycled thousands of miles! And in the summer, we'd hike. I liked looking at all the different flora and fauna.

'I loved everything I did, whatever it was. But that was me all of my life. I've never really wanted to give up. I've always been a real country girl. I'm not a clever clogs, but I'd tackle anything.

'We were supposed to give our badges back, but I kept mine.'

Audrey Amy Cleaver

Born on 4 May 1929; joined the Women's Land Army in 1945

'I joined up because I simply fancied a change from the job I was doing. I worked on the assembly line of a local factory, Carr Fastener in Stapleford. It was low-skilled, boring war work.

'I went to the local labour exchange and the information was all there. I think I had heard of the Women's Land Army, but it hadn't registered as important or interesting or something I might want to do.

'I wasn't particularly looking to join any of the forces although I did fancy joining the ATS or WAF, especially when you saw them in uniform. But I think you had to be 18.

'I wanted a different job and to get away as I was unsettled at home. I was only 16. I do always wonder about the fact that no parent or adult had to agree to me joining the WLA or moving away alone. Yet, when I got married, while I was still under 21, I needed permission from my older brother!

'Anyway, I filled in a form at the employment office and then they wrote to me, telling me where to go and join. I think it might have been difficult to recruit women. Most wanted to be in the more glamourous-seeming other services. It was also viewed as men's work and "not for women".

'I didn't go far really, although it seemed like it! I was stationed at Bunny, a village in Nottinghamshire.

Land Girl, Audrey Cleaver

I travelled alone to the nearest train station which was Ruddington. You could apply for different posts and areas to go. I could have been a Lumber Jill I suppose.

'I didn't know anyone, but I was looking forward to being away from home. We lived in a big house on the outskirts of Bunny. It wasn't a purpose-built hostel, just a house that had been taken over, probably commandeered.

'There was someone in charge who allocated our jobs, and we were given a complete uniform. It really was of good quality when you think of the khaki serge the soldiers wore. We were given a green hat, khaki shirts, green tie, green jumper – although some had sleeveless ones – corduroy jodhpurs like breeches, brogue shoes, long, knee-length khaki socks and a khaki overcoat. We had to wear this uniform to church and on parades. We were also given short-sleeved shirts and twill, khaki-coloured dungarees. We had to supply our own underwear and night clothes.

'There were over 30 girls there, with two large bedrooms which housed 16 in each. We slept in bunk beds. There was also a bath – a proper bath, not a tin one that had to be filled with the kettle. But with thirty girls it could be weeks between baths, so you had to be quick to get in there.

'At first it was a bit overwhelming, with all these strangers and it was so noisy! But it was like an adventure and there was a great sense of belonging to the group of girls. Good friendships were made. There were lots of laughs.

'And you just got on with it – remember, you didn't sign up for a period of time like in the services, and you could leave at any time, so people did. They'd be there and then they'd be gone, left or gone to get married. You hoped they had a top bunk that you could claim for yourself! Being on the bottom bunk was horrible, as the mattresses sagged, and it seemed they'd fall in on you while you were asleep, and they creaked. Plus, imagine 16 girls snoring and mumbling in their sleep!

'But you see photos in books and all these nostalgic posters and fridge magnets that show rosy-cheeked girls driving tractors and operating machinery. We didn't, well, except perhaps one or two girls who pushed themselves forward. No, we did the manual work, filling the sacks with the grain out of the threshing machines, stacking the bales of corn sheaves into "stooks". We also planted and harvested potatoes. It really was hard,

Audrey with a group of
Land Girls and soldiers.

physical work, especially for a young townie! We were soon fit, though.

'We worked with farm hands and Italian prisoners of war from the camp at Ruddington. They came to work on the back of lorries. We worked on farms in all the surrounding areas and all the arable farms. We either cycled there or got lifts on the lorries, but oh, we did a lot of walking.

'I can't remember how much we got paid, but I probably earned more in the factory, and remember we had free board and lodging. We ate in a huge dining room and we had breakfast and the evening meal at the hostel. There must have been a cook and possibly help for her as we didn't have to cook. There was

Audrey with POW's on the farm.

always a rush to get there first and get the food, especially the food put out for lunchtime pack out. If you weren't down early in a morning it was all gone.

'We didn't have much contact with the farmers, and they were OK as far as I recall, but our contact came through the person in charge of us. She allocated where we went, presumably as requested by local farmers. So, in that sense there was a sort of hierarchy of Women's Land Army staff.

'The locals were fine with us, too. We mixed most nights in the pub, The Rancliffe Arms, and they probably bought us drinks. We didn't get travel passes like those in the services did, but if you were hitchhiking in your uniform, you always got a lift. People were kindly to us. I remember there was a curfew and we were supposed to be in for lights out, but we didn't always make it!

'Yes, I would do it all again. I had to become independent and very resilient quickly and had to learn to get on with others and sort of hold my own, fight my own corner. It was a bit like survival of the fittest in that you had to be first up to get the pack out food, first up and ready to get the decent bicycle that worked and even to get the decent pairs of wellies.

'I don't think people expected us to fail or anything, it was just a case of getting on with it. And we did. I don't think we were viewed at all like the armed services, though. We were still civilians and could leave at any time. And we didn't get any recognition. Look how long it took for us to get a medal. Many had died, and of those left, probably a lot of them didn't know you could apply for one. Then the memorial was paid for by donations.

'But the glamourised pictures, the local reenactments where the women have fitted uniforms in a suitable 'vintage' style, and, of course, the women in the films make Land Girls seem flighty and frivolous, diminishing them as an important group who played a very significant part in the war effort of both wars. You know there were plump land girls as well. We've been romanticised, that's what's happened.'

Kathleen Dodd

Born on 8 April 1925; joined the Women's Land Army in 1942

'I joined the Land Army when I was 17 years old. The first farm I was stationed on was in Rainham, Kent. There were six of us all billeted in a house on the main road. I can remember the girls – there were two sisters from Liverpool, Ada Bull from London, Iris from Woolwich and Alma Williams from Chalk, Kent.

'It was quite hectic. We had to set off at 6am to Wakeley's farm, just through Rainham towards Sittingbourne. We all made a hell of a noise walking in our boots down the road, but there wasn't much traffic because of the shortage of petrol. If anything passed us it was usually army lorries.

'We weren't fed well really, but breakfast each morning was porridge, and we were given a lunch tin everyday with paste sandwiches in it. These

Kathleen Dodd.

were mostly thrown over the hedge as we walked to work! But not far from the farm was a transport café that we went into and bought egg and chips or sausage, so we were never hungry.

'Our first job there was cutting down waist-high weeds in the orchards. There was a man who helped called Bill, a bachelor. That poor man! What he had to put up with from us girls. He was forever sharpening our britching hooks which were a curved shape. He was quite kind to us, and often gave us a swig of his cold tea from his bottle.

'The farmer also had us cleaning up the farmyard and stables around the shire horses – they were damn great horses. We all had a try climbing on the backs of them of course, but we had to climb up on a stepladder. This was quite a laugh. Next, we had to pick up potatoes behind a tractor, a back-aching job.

'And if it rained, we were put in an underground storage area and had to inspect large cooking apples. Those with speckles on them were thrown into a large pit. The farmer told us we could take what we wanted, so at the weekend I took a case-full home, but they were so heavy that I didn't bother to take any home again. It was a pity as my mother would have made some lovely pies with them or passed some on to the neighbours.

'There was a field of golden gooseberries that had to be picked very carefully too, to be sent up to London in baskets. They were nearly as big as a chicken's egg. I'd never tasted or seen any like it since!

'Haymaking was next, and all of us enjoyed that, although it was hot, dirty, thirsty work. We were all taken by horse and cart along the main road towards Sittingbourne and sitting behind those big horses when they broke wind took your breath away. We had to walk up and down these fields turning the hay over to dry in the sun.

'During this time, we often stood watching "Dog fights" overhead with our Spitfires having a go at the German planes. We didn't realise just how serious things were in those days. At night the bombers used to go over to bomb Chatham Dockyards, so the searchlights and guns were always at it.

'The next day, we had to pitchfork the hay up into haycarts, and we would work each evening until 9pm, until the fields were cleared. Our foreman had a barrel of cider on his cart! I don't like cider really but drank some anyway as it was such thirsty work.

'We picked cherries too. These were large black ones called "naps" and tasted lovely. But we must have eaten more than we picked for the farmer! The trees were high, and the branches brittle, so we often fell into the trees, and I didn't like heights. We ate too many of these naps and had to go to the loo often! And the ladders were so high it took some time climbing up and down.

'Hop picking time was great, too. I had a long pole with a big hook knife on the top to cut the string, then we carried the hops to the local women that stood at their bins to pick them off. These women were very generous to us. They gave us cups of tea and at the end of the season gave us good tips, which we mostly spent on our midday meals at the Transport café! It was quite interesting going into the oast houses, the smell of drying hops was lovely.

'At the end of the summer season we were all sent to different farms. I went to a small farm with about six milking cows. It was in Beringrave Lane in Rainham and run by an old lady and man who could have been brother or sister or husband and wife. They were a funny old couple though, and they didn't have much to say to me. I think I was their first Land Army girl.

'On my first day, my job was in the barn on this contraption turning a damn great wheel – it was like a mincer, putting turnips in for the cow-feed. The cows kept coming into the barn, wanting me to feed them and I kept shooing them away. What a boring job that was after working with five other girls. It was so quiet. Then the next day this little old dear said she would try me at milking and took me in the milking shed. She sat on a little, old, three-legged stool and started singing nursery rhymes while milking. Then she told me to have a go. I didn't get much milk out, perhaps I should have sung nursery rhymes.

'The cow kept swishing its tail around my face. I just couldn't get into milking, so I did a lot of muck clearing, and I had to get buckets of water and wash the stalls out with a broom. The cows had only to look at me and I backed off. Before the day was out, I had fallen backwards into the gully, got soaked and smelled of cows the rest of the day. I was so glad to get a good wash later on.

'In the farmyard there was a shed with a great bull chained through the ring in its nose, and I was forever worried it would get out as there were usually about 15 cows wandering around.

'I missed working with other Land Army girls though and asked for a move to a hostel. While I was waiting for a place, I was sent to a house at Bluebell Hill to do some greenhouse work. My digs were about half a mile from there. The bedroom had a single iron bedstead and a chair – not very nice.

'I didn't sleep much the first night there as it seemed to be running alive with fleas, and I went to work feeling quite tired. Then I was made to dig in this long garden, a really back-breaking job where I never saw anyone the whole day, and they didn't offer a drink of any kind. This place was an ex-mayor's house, as I saw these large portraits of men with chains around their neck in their lounge.

'The back garden where I worked had three long greenhouses which seemed endless. I still can't understand how a Land Army girl was sent there; it certainly was not farm work. I went back to my digs and packed my bag and went home to Gravesend. I sent a letter to the Land Army headquarters and asked again to be sent to a hostel with other girls.

'After a couple of days, they sent me to Ridley near Meopham. The hostel was at the back of Ridley church. It seemed a huge house, but I've since been to see it again and was so surprised to see it wasn't very big after all.

'It was great. My bedroom was in the attic and there were four of us in there. Our window overlooked the churchyard, and the first floor had the kitchens, dining area and a sitting room which contained an old piano. One of the girls could play all the tunes we needed, and we did some dancing! Some of the girls could jitterbug so the floorboards moved and cracked. We had lots of laughs. There seemed to be no heating in the house, so our bedroom was quite cold. I slept in my army socks, and we had plenty of blankets on our beds. There was a rush to get a wash in the bathrooms, because the hot water soon turned to cold, so I went home most weekends and had a good bath.

'The jobs here were mostly hoeing potatoes after the corn and haymaking was finished. We all enjoyed laughing and talking together as there were 21 of us at the hostel. We were invited to dances at the Officers Training Camp at Wrotham that they gave now and again. They would send a lorry to pick us all up and we sat on boxes in the back. There was always lots of food and some drink, and the band seemed quite good too. We were taken home before midnight as our hostel front door was locked on the dot of midnight. They were all a good bunch of lads. We had a good time there.

'Our meals in the hostel seemed quite good. Breakfast was mainly cornflakes, so if you didn't hurry to get up when the bell went there was no milk left. One morning I was hurrying and slipped down two flights of stairs. I had my thick socks on and there was no carpet on the stairs, but I just went flying down the first flight, around the corner and down the second lot of stairs. My bottom and head hurt, and they all stood laughing at me. I could not sit down properly for weeks. The hostel matron sent me to see the doctor at Meopham, which was very embarrassing, and I was sent for an x-ray. I was told I had bent my coccyx. I was supposed to go back to see the doctor but just could not face it. I still kept going, and I really think they didn't realise how bad my neck and back hurt.

'My husband, Arthur, proposed to me while walking around the lanes near the Ridley hostel, and after we got married, I left.'

Land girls enjoying a singalong. (*Wikimedia*)

Rosalind Scott showing
a farmer her WLA band.
(*Wikimedia*)

Soldiers helping Land Girls with the harvest, July 1945. (*Wikimedia*)

Lumberjill training camp at Culford. (*Wikimedia*)

Gunners running past WLA members. (*Wikimedia*)

Three Land Girls on
the British home front.
(*Wikimedia*)

Harvesting at Mount
Barton, Devon 1942.
(*Wikimedia*)

Land Girl Dorothy
Sills. (*Wikimedia*)

Land Girls on
a dairy farm in
Norfolk, 1944.
(*Wikimedia*)

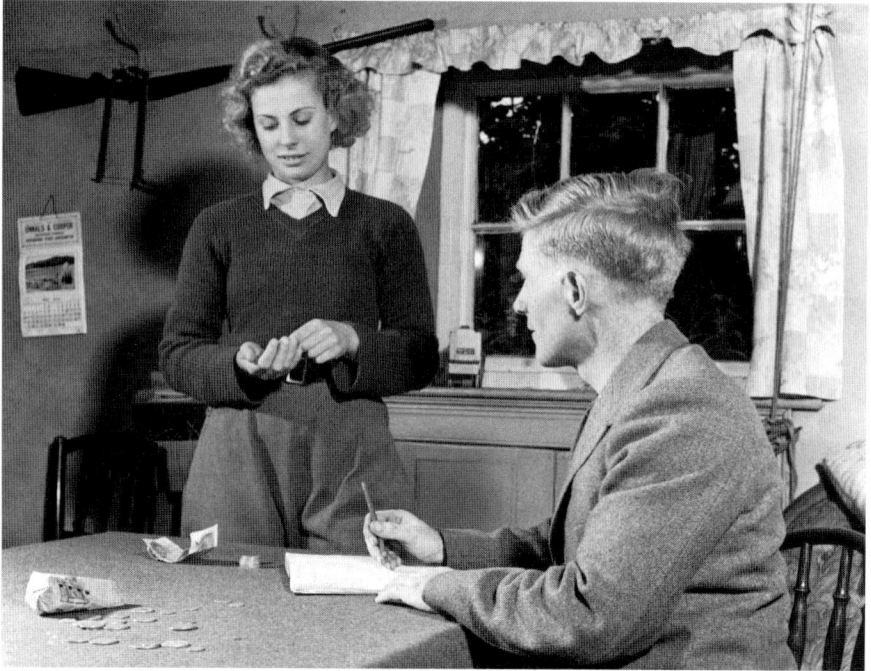

Land Girl Iris Joyce getting paid. (*Wikimedia*)

Land Girl preparing
rat poison as part
of their training in
Suffolk in 1942.
(*Wikimedia*)

'I Wonder'

Barbara Barton, East Riding of Yorkshire

I wonder if crows
Get cramp in their toes
As they suddenly land with a flop;
And I wonder if worms
Ever have any qualms
As they hastily enter the crop.
Perhaps the birds learn
That even worms turn
As they rapidly pass out of sight,
Poor crows, do they suffer
From those who are tougher?
They mightn't – who knows – but they might.
I wonder if bees
Ever happen to sneeze
When the pollen gets into their noses?
I wonder if ants
Can enjoy a romance?
They put work before love, one supposes.
I wonder if moles
Get bored in their holes
And want to go gay like the rest?
Do they train centipedes
To guide them on leads?
I wonder – does *Nature* know best?

Mary Davies

Born on 16 September 1923; joined the Women's Land Army in 1942
'If I am truthful, my overall memory is of very hard work, but I can honestly say that I loved my four years as a Land Girl.

'I joined in 1942, after leaving my position as assistant warden at the YHA climbing hostel in North Wales – Idwal Cottage – at the end of the Ogwen Valley. During my first week at the hostel a young student from Liverpool University fell to his death while tackling one of the most difficult climbs. When a tragedy like that happens to someone so young, it makes such an impression and I decided that I wouldn't stay for the whole winter. So, in January, I left the hostel to join all the Land Girls helping on farms.

'I worked on a mixed farm on the edge of Shrewsbury, for the princely wage of £1 per week plus board, rising to £1.50 in 1944. These days that sum sounds pitiful, but I was working such long hours I still somehow managed to save. I opened my first bank account with £10 and felt so rich!

'I began work at 6.30am assisting with the milking, all done by hand, and it wasn't until a year or so later that a machine was installed. Breakfast normally followed, then it was back to the cow houses for mucking out, laying clean, fresh bedding of straw and leaving fodder of hay for the cows to come back in to.

'The hardest thing was climbing the ladder to cut hay off. It was stacked loose and once wedges were cut, it had to be brought backwards down the ladder on a pitchfork. When a strong wind was blowing, I found this particularly difficult and many times I couldn't hold on to my load. One day I was reduced to tears of frustration, but there was no one to witness, or to help.

'My 21st birthday fell in September and my parents wrote to say that they were looking forward to seeing me and would expect me for lunch. I told my employer and his response was, "yes, after you have finished your work though".

'So, I set off on the 12-mile cycle ride to my home, was showered with gifts and had a delicious lunch with my parents. I believe it was roast partridge, which came into season in September. I told them that I had to go back to the farm at 2:30pm because I had to be back for afternoon milking. My parents were hopping mad, saying, "surely you don't have to leave?" But I did and off I went!

'The other thing I vividly remember is that each Autumn, when it was time for the potatoes to be harvested, a family of gypsies arrived. They came in a horse-drawn caravan and stayed for several weeks. The potatoes were lifted with a horse-drawn plough and it was back-breaking work to pick all of them.

'I used to love chatting to the gypsies and just watching them, as their way of life was so fascinating. They were, however, strangely very fond of eating hedgehogs and after they were caught and killed, they were coated with a layer of thick mud, and roasted on the embers of a wood fire. When the mud casing was peeled off, all of the spikes came with it and the hedgehog was ready for eating. Apparently, it tasted delicious, though I can assure you, I never sampled it!'

Violet May Edwards

An excerpt originally found in 'The Women's Land Army'

Born on 22 February 1929; joined the Women's Land Army in 1949
'I was born in North London and had worked in toy, sweet and metal box factories, as well as in a greengrocer's and as a cinema usherette before joining up. I had seen the recruitment posters and thought, this is for me. But the first time I tried to join the Women's Land Army my father put a stop to it by previously informing the recruitment office that I was underage. I was very mad because it made me look like a fool!

'I persevered, though, and finally trained in basic farming skills on Brigg farm in Lincolnshire. Once trained, I undertook a range of farm work such as haymaking, picking potatoes and pulling sugar beet and carrots. I ploughed too, and fed the pigs and horses and mucked them out. I think my favourite work was driving the tractor and pulling carrots. My least? Definitely digging potatoes.

'I lived in a hostel at Saxilby, Lincolnshire. I met some lovely women, and I have only good memories of the friends and happy times in the Women's Land Army. I remember one time a gang of us Land Girls were pulling carrots in a field at the side of a road. It was a hot summer's day and some of the girls had stripped down to their bras. We noticed a car had parked up at the side of the road and stayed for a long time. One of the girls said, "he's watching us" and set off to circle behind the car. We saw her reach the car with her arms waving, then saw the car speeding off. "A dirty old man with binoculars!" she said, as she strode back across the field!

'I left just before the WLA was disbanded and married my husband, Jack, in 1950, an ex-solider from the village in Saxilby. We first met when he came to the Land Army hostel to meet another land girl. She didn't want to go out with him so sent me to the door to tell him. Jack said, will

Violet with her Land Girl friends.

Violet lived in a Land Girl
hostel in Lincolnshire.

WOMEN'S LAND ARMY (ENGLAND & WALES)

RELEASE CERTIFICATE

The Women's Land Army for England and Wales acknowledges
with appreciation the services given by

VIOLET BUDD

who has been an enrolled member for the period from

12th August 1949 to 1st September 1950

and has this day been granted a willing release.

Date 1.9.50.

W. Heppenstall

WOMEN'S LAND ARMY

you come out with me instead? I felt sorry for him and then followed over 62 years of marriage!

'We spent the first seven years as husband and wife living in a single decker bus, followed by four years in a caravan as Jack worked as a heavy plant driver and fitter on open-cast and excavation sites around the country. He would often come back to the bus at night and say pack up we are moving to the next job. Hard work in the WLA helped prepare for a hard life.'

Muriel Hughes

Born on 23 July 1919; joined the Women's Land Army 1939
'I joined the Women's Land Army straight away, working on several different farms from Herefordshire on the Radnorshire Border and then in Monmouthshire up on The Sugar Loaf, before ending up on a farm near Llanfapley where I met my husband.

'Oh, I have some stories! Dances in village halls, local farm lads and their behaviour, Italians who, no, I didn't like, and German prisoners of war who I did feel a bit sorry for and they worked hard. The only thing I think I ever complained bitterly about was the much-needed boots for the girls which didn't arrive for weeks after we started. Working in deep mud and manure without them was beyond tough. Apart from that I took to the job heartily.

'One of my most memorable moments was when a carthorse needed to be shod, but it was three miles to the farrier at Lanes Llanvetherine and I

Muriel Hughes with a working horse.

had to lead the mare. It was a long, hot walk and the mare wasn't keen as she had left a foal behind. Once shod, I decided that a nice, quiet 'rocking' plod home atop this lovely mare would be very pleasant and I scrambled on up. But the mare had other ideas – she had a foal at home! So I had to hold on tight as the mare made very good time on the way back with me, this terrified rider, still on her back, white with tears of fear still dripping from my chin on arrival back near Llanddewi Rhydderch.

'I loved the fresh air, the nature, the animals and just being outside. It was such a change for a young girl born within the sound of Bow Bells! I never went back to London except to visit.'

Lilian Taylor

Born on 16 April 1924; joined the Women's Land Army in 1942
'I went to school on City Road, Manchester. My parents had a pub, but my mother died when I was 12 and my father died on my 15th birthday, so my step-brother took the pub over. But me and my sister stayed there until we were married.

'Before the war I worked in a milliner's in Manchester. I was like an apprentice, learning how to stitch and modelling the hats. There were about 20 of us who worked there, for about 9 shillings and 8 pence a week. I was only 14. Then I went to work in a factory that made folders.

'My father didn't have a lot of money, and when my mum died we had to do the cleaning in the house because he could not afford to pay someone else to do it. It was a very poor area, Hulme. You were lucky if you got to go to the pictures and it was only a shilling back then.

'I remember Chamberlain's broadcast. During the war, I was frightened of the air raids and we used to go in the cellar. My sister-in-law had a baby and we used to wrap her in an eiderdown for fear of anything happening.

'I remember once, I went out for tea with a friend and her boyfriend one night. It was the night of the Manchester blitz. The sirens went, and my friend's boyfriend said that he must get home as his mother was on her own, and we had to run through the streets, dodging in doorways – all the glass from the windows were breaking. I've never been as frightened.

'We got to the road where the pub was and all the houses had been pulled down, but just as we got in the middle of it the sky absolutely lit up – it was like daylight. My friend's boyfriend shouted, "Get down for your life!" We both lay down and he put himself across both of us. All of a sudden the lights went out and he said to run because they used to drop explosives once they had dropped incendiaries. I cut all my knees and my friend cut all her head. We were shaking. I just managed to get home and we went into the cellar and stayed there all night.

'After the Manchester blitz it calmed down and I went into the Land Army. I was about 18 or 19, and you had to register for work or the forces. I went to Dover street in Manchester to join The Women's Auxiliary Air Force, but I had deformed toes and they would not accept me. They told me to go to Princess Street where the Land Army were recruiting. I went straight there, signed on and within a month I got the uniform and the lot – shirt, big breeches, stockings, overcoat and brogues.

'I trained in Staffordshire for a month and from there they sent me to Carnforth to a farm where there was only one farmer and his sister. But I did not like him. I could not get on with him. We would to go into the fields collecting stones and he used to turn his back on me and make water. Well, with me being a town girl I was disgusted, you know.

'I used to be frightened to death in a morning when he would come and wake me up at 5:30 am and there was no lock on the door. We would get up, get washed and milk the cows. He had about 12 and had to hand milk them and then go back for breakfast. I was a bit scared of milking at first because the animals were moving, but I can milk a cow as well as anybody. Well, I could then, I don't know about now!

'Anyway, a lady used to come and make sure we were happy where we were staying and I then got billeted with an elderly lady in her seventies in Lymm, Cheshire, and my friend was in the same house. I was there until I came out of the Land Army.

'We used to do haymaking, potato picking, planting cabbages – just general farming. It did take a bit of getting used to. I can remember one morning while we were in the boiler house changing into our boots for the fields, a man came and said scatter the bulls loose! I also remember taking a pig to be served with a boar and I had to go on a 20-minute walk down the road with this pig. I got to the level crossing and she would not go. Imagine it – she was a big sow! I tried all sorts to get her across. I liked the farmer there, but he got injured by a bull. It ripped all his skin on his thigh, and he was out of work for nine weeks.

There was a pub nearby and we used to go dancing there every Friday night and the Americans would come. Then at the weekend I used to go home and go dancing at Old Trafford!

'I was not married until after the war, but I was friends with my husband, John, throughout. I did not, however, hear from him for a long time, and thought he had got someone else so did not bother writing, but what I did not know was that he was going through Normandy.

'When the war ended, I had been in the fields all day and had gone home. I was really tired, and it took me about an hour-and-a-half to get home, so it was midnight. My sister came up and said, "come on were going to Albert's square, the wars ended!" But I turned over I said I couldn't go as I was too tired! But there was singing and dancing in the square.

'I can remember nearly everything that happened in the war and my years in the Land Army. I was in there for four years and I really enjoyed it. We had some upsets, but on the whole I really enjoyed it.

'I did all sorts. You couldn't go to the loo or anything like – you had to go in a ditch and the fellas used to whistle to tell you they were coming! And when we were muck spreading, there was like a wagon on the back loaded up with manure. We used to stand on it while they were scattering it in the fields.

'One time I can remember while threshing, one of the chaps was feeding the threshing machine, and on this day we were singing away, but all of a sudden he said, "quick go and get somebody!" When I came back, a rat had jumped down his shirt and he had had to grab it before it bit him.

'There were one or two accidents. The farmer's daughter, Alice, was in charge of the dairy and you used to wash the udders before the machine went on and one kicked out at her. It hit her full in the face and knocked her teeth out.

'We used to feed the calves that would not suckle, and the pigs, if they farrowed, we had to move the babies because you know, they would squish them to death. I used to love haymaking and harvesting. It was damn hard work, but I really enjoyed it.

'When I came home, I just got used to town life again, and John came out at the same time. He just looked at me and said, "hello" and said he would come down to the pub, and that is how we got courting again.'

'The Old Labourer'

Daphne Hudson, Essex

You're a stacker now –
Up there with my old fork in your hands.
You've got a pair of hands that understands,
Though last year that old fork still worked in mine.
Worked fine,
As it always did
Back down that old stairway of time.
This June ain't as any other June.
You make the hay without me
And, come harvest,
You'll pitch the sheaves
Easy as dropped leaves
As I could once
When the blood still ran true and free
In the frame that was me.
Now, the rain that fell
Over four-score years and ten
On fields and men
Has gotten right in where the movement came
And stopped the game,
The game of living.
Now I can only watch you,
Being me,
So like-so like,
I live again,
Young and strong and free.

The Lost Women

It was only in 2008 that the government awarded a badge of honour to over 45,000 former Land Girls, and The Prince of Wales unveiled a memorial dedicated to the women who served in The Women's Land Army during the First and Second World Wars.

Many did not live to receive the award, but a large number of Land Girls I have spoken to did not express any anger or resentment at the fact this recognition came over 70 years too late.

Even my own grandmother was reluctant to send off the form to apply for the badge. It was me, in fact, who did so, and I have her badge to this day. It was as if she did not need anything tangible to prove her years of service; she had her memories, her stories, her strength.

This the Women's Land Army and Women's Timber Corps memorial. (*Wikimedia*)

Only at rare times did a glimmer of upset or bitterness come from those I have interviewed, only to be quickly squashed as their stories continued, speaking of more important factors such as the friendships or relationships formed during their service.

We shall never know the hardships that the war generation faced, nor the fear they lived with, but we owe them the honour of remembrance. It is now our duty as we move forwards to educate, share and celebrate the generation who gave their lives in many ways for our freedom. And for that, we continue to thank you.

We will remember you.